12/16

D0391418

THE
AMERICAN
DREAM
REVISITED

GARY SIRAK

NASHVILLE

NEW YORK MELBOURNE

THE AMERICAN DREAM REVISITED
ORDINARY PEOPLE, EXTRAORDINARY RESULTS

Published in New York, New York, by Morgan James Publishing. Morgan James and The Entrepreneurial Publisher are trademarks of Morgan James, LLC.
www.MorganJamesPublishing.com

The Morgan James Speakers Group can bring authors to your live event. For more information or to book an event visit The Morgan James Speakers Group at www.TheMorganJamesSpeakersGroup.com.

Shelfie

A **free** eBook edition is available
with the purchase of this print book.

CLEARLY PRINT YOUR NAME ABOVE IN UPPER CASE

Instructions to claim your free eBook edition:
1. Download the Shelfie app for Android or iOS
2. Write your name in **UPPER CASE** above
3. Use the Shelfie app to submit a photo
4. Download your eBook to any device

ISBN 978-1-63047-963-3 paperback
ISBN 978-1-63047-964-0 casebound
ISBN 978-1-63047-965-7 eBook
Library of Congress Control Number:
2016901387

Cover Design by:
Ryan Humbert

Cover Layout & Interior Design by:
Megan Whitney
Creative Ninja Designs
megan@creativeninjadesigns.com

In an effort to support local communities, raise awareness and funds, Morgan James Publishing donates a percentage of all book sales for the life of each book to Habitat for Humanity Peninsula and Greater Williamsburg.

Get involved today! Visit
www.MorganJamesBuilds.com

Table of
CONTENTS

PREFACE

The stories in *The American Dream Revisited* are based on people whom I have had the good fortune to come in contact with throughout my lifetime. I have found their journeys to be both inspirational and enlightening and I thank them from the bottom of my heart for agreeing to be a part of this book. All quotations are taken directly from my interviews and conversations with each subject, and my hope is that their stories will inspire you to seek your own American Dream.

Gary Sirak

For additional information on *The American Dream Revisited* or author Gary Sirak please visit www.GarySirak.com.

FOREWORD

The American Dream.

Few terms engender as much interest, imagination, and inspiration whenever it's referred to or comes up in conversation. Indeed, the American Dream is one of the enduring elements of Americana; it's part of what President Reagan referred to as " … that beacon light that guides freedom-loving people everywhere."

Although first popularized in the 1931 book, "Epic of America," by James Truslow Adams, The American Dream originated in the minds of seekers of opportunity centuries ago. Surely the names on the Mayflower manifest were those of the dreamers of a new life so precious they were willing to risk everything to make it come true. And so they did.

The signers of the Declaration of Independence, by then with more evidence to justify their risks, surely valued the idea of an American Dream. When they signed their names to a document including inspired concepts such as, "… life, liberty and the pursuit of happiness …", and the passion to " … mutually pledge to each other our lives, our fortunes and our sacred honor," they were signing onto the American Dream. And, four score and seven years later, Lincoln still referred to what we now call the American Dream as an experiment.

Isn't that the beauty of it? The evidence is different with each generation, and yet the ideal still captivates us enough to continue our pursuit.

My friend Gary Sirak and I agree that the American Dream is more of a force than just an idea. It may be unique among intangibles in that it actually becomes something you can hold when applied in an environment where freedom flourishes. Freedom comes from God. Liberty is a contract we give to each other. No other ideal flowers in the fertile soil of liberty like the American Dream. There is no English Dream. No German Dream. No Chinese Dream.

And warts and all, bloom it does—as Gary reveals in his new book, *The American Dream Revisited.*

Underpinned by demonstrations of courage and perseverance, the American Dream is alive and well in the stories Gary tells. You'll be encouraged, uplifted and motivated to reset your quest. This is a very real and unique mindset that has become the manifestation of the passion, risk, sacrifice and love by those who built and bequeathed this country to us, and upon whose shoulders we now stand. And throughout The American Dream Revisited, Gary shows you the formula you can use to claim it yourselves.

America may never be perfect, but on the balance sheet of nations, it has been much more benevolent, generous and inspiring than any other in history. Thanks Gary, for helping us not lose sight of that. In a few short pages, you'll be thanking Gary too.

Jim Blasingame
Leading expert on small business and entrepreneurship
Author of the award-winning book, *The Age of the Customer*
Host of "The Small Business Advocate Show"

NOTE TO READER

A morning visit to a coffee shop kept Gary Sirak up all night—and it wasn't because of the caffeine. It was something he'd overheard: four college students discussing The American Dream. Except, they referred to it as The American *Disaster*.

Sirak disagreed so much that he literally couldn't sleep that night. Rising and writing, he wrote a response in the form of 13 stories about people whose real-life American Dreams have taken them from surviving to thriving.

The first story he tells is his own. Growing up one of six people in a house built for three, Sirak watched as his father worked two jobs just to make ends meet. One job his father loved, and one he despised. But with persistence came the family's first new car and a house where Gary could have his own room.

Eventually there was even money for Sirak to attend college, where he enrolled in an American Literature course. The readings had themes of the American Dream: freedom, opportunity and class struggle. The professor stoked debate: was the American Dream, like their books, fiction, or something real? For Sirak, the answer was always "real."

The people he met later proved him right. It is their stories that came to Sirak's mind in the middle of the night: an Amish man turned construction entrepreneur, a South African immigrant turned small business owner, an arts administrator who turned a community around, and more.

In the end, *The American Dream Revisited* is an anthem for an age of uncertainty, a reminder that hard work and determination still matter, and a promise that the American Dream is about more than buying the things we want; it is about becoming the people we want to be.

1 WHY I WROTE THIS BOOK

"Mostly brilliant, not sure why you don't put this much thought and effort into every assignment. Sometimes, Gary, you lack focus."

I vividly remembered those words, written by my high school English teacher, Mrs. Giltz, next to the A on one of my assignments. The timing for recalling her mostly positive comments was good. It was 1969, my first day at Miami University in Oxford, Ohio, and I had to register for classes and declare a major.

I was clueless as to what choices to make until I recalled Mrs. Glitz's words. I decided to focus on the "mostly" part of brilliant and discount my occasional lack of focus. I declared

English as my major with an emphasis on American literature. That decision led me on a path to my introduction and subsequent lifelong fascination with the American Dream.

One of my first English classes was an American literature survey course taught by Professor James G. Denham. Every week we read a novel by a famous author: Kurt Vonnegut, Joseph Heller, Sinclair Lewis, and F. Scott Fitzgerald, to name a few. Professor Denham focused our weekly classroom discussions on the American Dream and how it was portrayed in each novel. He was witty, had a wry sense of humor and relished our classroom discussions. He loved to incite arguments—pro and con—regarding the American Dream. Professor Denham would build a case for the dream's existence or non-existence and then let us students battle it out.

The memory brought a smile to my face which faded rapidly after one of the students referred to the American Dream as the American disaster.

Seventy-five percent of the class felt the American Dream was already history. The anti-dream sentiment was not surprising considering what was happening throughout the United States in 1969. As students, we protested the Viet Nam War, a mandatory armed forces draft, and women's rights. The unsettling political atmosphere that existed on campus was also reflected in our classroom.

In spite of my support regarding the aforementioned protests, I found myself in the minority in Professor Denham's class. I argued that the American Dream was still relevant, debating with passion and even anger during some of our discussions. The funny thing is I never knew the origin of my passion until I started writing *The American Dream Revisited*. In chapter 3 you will learn why I take the American Dream so personally.

Fast forward forty years. I was sipping a mocha at Karma Café, one of my favorite coffee shops in Canton, Ohio. It was early in the morning and I was looking over my schedule for what I expected to be a busy day when four university students sat down at the table behind me. Quite by accident, I overheard a discussion that piqued my interest.

The students were talking about the American Dream and whether or not it existed. Just like that *déjà vu* set in. I flashed back to Professor Denham and my college class in the late '60s. The smile that memory brought to my face rapidly faded after one of the students referred to the American Dream as the American Disaster. Two of his friends agreed with him, calling the Dream irrelevant and dead. Ironically, it was three against one, the same split as in my American literature class many years prior. I wanted to join their discussion and it took all the restraint I could muster not to pull my chair up to their table, but I wisely resisted and just listened. The three argued the United States was no longer a land of opportunity, but a land of disappointment. Their reasons were college debt and a tight job market. The fourth student at the table agreed his college loans were a problem, but just an obstacle he could overcome once he graduated and went to work. He attempted to explain his plan but never got the chance. His friends refused to listen. After a while they tired of the topic and switched conversational gears, at which point I tuned out.

I left Karma Café that morning with some very bad karma. My intention of sipping my mocha and getting focused for work was destroyed. The students' conversation disturbed me. Here were three future college graduates with their entire lives ahead of them and they had already given up. I could not let go of their conversation. It even invaded my sleep. During one of my restless nights, I decided to fight back and began planning *The American Dream Revisited; Ordinary People, Extraordinary Results.*

My goal is simple. I want to inspire as many people as I can to explore the opportunities and possibilities that exist in their lives. I firmly believe the American Dream is still alive, well, and living in the United States.

So grab a cup of coffee from your favorite coffee shop and join me on my journey in search of the American Dream—and some good karma!

[
The power of encouragement cannot be overlooked. It has been so important for me throughout my life. Without question Mrs. Giltz's notation on my paper proved inspirational and for that I am thankful.
]

2
AN HISTORIC
PERSPECTIVE

I admit it. I am guilty as charged.

My crime is that every Friday night, I—along with seven million other viewers—watch the reality television show, S*hark Tank*. The show, which debuted in 2009, invites entrepreneurs to present their products and ideas to a panel of highly-successful, self-made business men and women. I enjoy the creativity of the entrepreneurial contestants as they attempt to convince one of the millionaire/billionaire "sharks" to invest in their ideas. The show is well produced with dramatic music, suspenseful time-outs, spirited banter, and competition among the sharks to close a deal. Those entrepreneurs lucky enough to appear on Shark Tank and join forces with one of the sharks receive expert business advice, financial backing, and impressive connections. The sharks and contestants often reference the American Dream when describing their efforts to make it in the business world.

Shark Tank may be giving voice to the American Dream in the twenty-first century, but it was Horatio Alger in the nineteenth century who first popularized the concept.

In 1865, Alger wrote a series of stories for a youth magazine called *Student and Schoolmate.* The stories were so successful that Alger compiled them into his first and most famous novel, *Ragged Dick: Or Street Life in New York with the Boot Blacks.* His book's impact was twofold. On one hand, Alger focused on the uplifting, rags-to-riches story of the main character, Dick, a poor shoeshine boy living on the streets, earning pennies by shining boots. Dick bettered his life through hard work, determination, courage, honesty, and luck. The book also drew attention to a social problem plaguing New York City. Thousands of abandoned youth were homeless, starving, and living on the streets. The popularity of *Ragged Dick* caused a public outcry that forced New York City to take action. With religious organizations leading the way, the homeless youth of the city began to receive food, clothing, and shelter.

Ironically, even though Alger spent his life writing about the American Dream, he never named it as such.

Critics panned Alger's work for being simplistic and repetitive, but he went on to write over a hundred books with the common theme of self-improvement through education, strong morals and hard work. Alger became one of the most popular and successful authors of his time. His novels were instant best sellers and inspired millions of readers to improve their own lives.

Ironically, even though Alger spent his life writing about the American Dream, he never named it as such. The term first appeared in print in 1931 in *The Epic of America*, by James Truslow Adams, an American author and historian. He named and defined the American Dream as: "That dream of a land in which life should be better and richer and fuller for everyone, with opportunity for each according to ability or achievement… regardless of the fortuitous circumstances of birth or position."

I believe for many people the stories of achieving great success and wealth depicted on *Shark Tank* epitomizes today's definition of the American Dream. The opportunity to become rich is certainly a popular aspect of the American Dream but it's not the whole story, not by a long shot. The popular show may give an illusion of overnight success, but success is more often found through a combination of hard work, a determination to overcome adversity, and a belief in yourself and your abilities.

The American Dream Revisited is a collection of stories about people who have achieved success in their lives and who serve as examples of the American Dream.

I think Alger would be amazed at how his simple stories have lived on via the Horatio Alger Society and the millions of dollars in scholarships they have awarded to students who have overcome adversity in their lives.

3
A PERSONAL
PERSPECTIVE

A double cheeseburger, french-fries with a pad of butter on top, and a hot fudge milkshake was what I ordered at Heggy's Nut Shop the day I met Barry Adelman for lunch. He and I have been friends since we were little kids. Barry is one of my favorite people to talk to when something is on my mind and my American Dream Karma Café experience certainly fit the bill. I mentioned how it disturbed me to overhear comments like the American Dream now being the American Disaster. I told Barry I'd decided to write a book to prove them wrong. He thought it was a good idea. It was at that point during lunch when I made a confession. "Barry, for the life of me I have no idea why that conversation bothered me so much. I mean, why do I even care?"

Barry smiled and answered, "You don't really get it, do you? For a smart guy sometimes you are not that smart."

"Ok, enlighten me; what am I missing?"

"Gary, it is because you are too close to your past. Your father could have been the proverbial poster child for the American Dream. You need to write the story of your family and include it in your book."

There it was. The *ah-ha* moment. For the first time in my life I now understood why I cared so much about the American Dream and the origin of my passion. So, as Barry suggested, I offer my personal story of someone who personifies the American Dream. Meet my father, Stan Sirak.

I grew up in Canton, Ohio, in a crowded house on 37th Street. Our family of four lived in a home designed for three. It got much smaller when my mother's father, Daniel Factor, moved in with us. The house shrunk even more when my sister was born and the small den was converted into her nursery. Six of us were now living in a home built for half as many. My father desperately wanted to fix the problem but that would have meant moving to a larger house and that would have cost money, something that was in short supply in my family.

My father was all too familiar with living through tough times. His mother passed away from breast cancer when he was just eleven years old. His father, Abraham Sirak, was left with the dual responsibility of raising three young children and earning a living. Grandpa Abe was a dentist and provided a decent living for his family, but that changed when he shifted his focus from his practice to finding a new wife and a mother for his children. His quest for a spouse was made much more challenging because his daughter was legally blind and required special attention. Grandpa Abe began what amounted to a state-wide search, moving from Cincinnati to Canton and eventually to Toledo. Although the moves were calculated, the constant relocation was extremely stressful for my father and his siblings. They were never able to establish long-term friends or a sense of community. Another unintended consequence to the constant moving was that it was virtually impossible for Grandpa Abe to rebuild a dental practice. Money was tight.

In my opinion there were additional contributing factors in Grandpa Abe's inability to reestablish his practice. He was gruff, had a poor chair-side manner, and lacked outward compassion for his patients' pain; not great qualities for a dentist. On the marriage front, Grandpa Abe was nothing if not persistent. He married and divorced four times in his search to find a suitable mother and wife. This was my father's reality, a far cry from a stable childhood.

My other grandfather, Dan Factor, was an entrepreneur who owned one of the most successful beer and wine distribution companies on the East Coast. Following World War II and his service in the Navy, my father went to work in his father-in-law's company. He was the number one salesman but never seemed to get much respect from my grandfather. Daniels Distributing

Company flourished until my grandfather got distracted by his new found wealth and started making a series of poor business decisions. My father pleaded with Grandpa Dan to let him take over the daily operations of the company but my grandfather's ego stood in the way. He let my father know it was his company and he was going to manage it his way. Unfortunately, Grandpa Dan's poor decisions resulted in the ultimate failure and closure of Daniel Distributing. The end result was Grandpa Dan moving into our small home and my father being unemployed.

My father was offered jobs from other companies in the beer and wine industry but he turned down those opportunities because he was tired of spending so much time in bars. His goal was to find a new career that allowed him to be his own boss.

After an extended search, my father accepted a job selling life insurance. This turned out to be a very difficult way to earn a living, as selling an intangible product was much different than selling beer and wine. When I later asked Dad how he chose a career in the insurance industry, he replied: "It was an easy decision; it was my only offer that did not require me to travel, I believed in the product, and I thought I could help people." The insurance company paid him a minimal salary to get started and then it was one hundred percent commission-based. Dad got off to a very slow start and the insurance company wanted to fire him, but fortunately my father's sales manager saw his potential and persuaded the company to be patient.

To supplement his income, Dad found weekend employment selling shoes. To say that he hated this job would not really do justice to how he really felt. Every Saturday morning my father would leave the house in a bad mood and return in an even worse mood. He would throw whatever money he had earned on the kitchen table and loudly remind everyone just how much he despised dealing with people's feet. I think he washed his hands a dozen times before he would sit down to dinner.

One of my earliest memories of my mother and father was of the two of them sitting at the kitchen table with stacks of envelopes. Mom was in charge of managing the family finances and paying bills. They would sit for hours trying to determine what bills they had to pay and who they could stall. I learned that the farther away I was from the kitchen the better off I would be. These were not good discussions and they never had a happy ending, just frustration and a stack of unpaid bills.

It was 1964 and strange things began happening on 37th Street.

After seven lean years selling insurance, Dad's passion and hard work began to pay off. He had become a student of the industry and earned licenses, certifications, and knowledge that set him apart from many competitors. It was 1964 and strange things began happening on 37th Street. One evening my father pulled into the driveway in a new car. The family car was old and had seen better days. Shopping for a new automobile was often a dinner table topic of discussion that always ended with my father saying, "Someday when we have more money." On this particular evening the whole family climbed into the new car for a test drive. Dad was in a great mood and after a short while asked each of us for an opinion regarding the automobile. My response, "It is nice but is the ugliest shade of green that I have ever seen," caused my father to laugh so hard he had to pull off the road to catch his breath.

Another indication that something was going on occurred when our test drive ended up at Taggert's Ice Cream Parlor. It was the first time I remember the family going out for ice cream. It was a big deal and I still smile today whenever I go to Taggert's for a cone. Also worth noting, Dad returned the ugly green car and picked out a really pretty blue one. Who knows, maybe my comment about the color carried more weight than I thought.

The following Saturday morning dad did not go to the shoe store. He announced that he no longer needed to sell shoes and that we were going out to dinner to celebrate. Everyone dressed up and we went to one of the nicest restaurants in Canton. The dinner discussion that evening was different. My parents talked about goal setting, achieving goals, and celebrating victories. It was way over my head but I sure liked the celebration part. Life in the Sirak household became way more fun and it seemed as though we were always celebrating something.

As my dad became more successful, my parents began a search for a new home. I was not happy. Even as a young kid I was very set in my ways, did not like change, and was apprehensive about leaving our crowded home. My negative attitude changed quickly when I learned that I would have my own bedroom. Moving to the new home was a great improvement in our family's quality of life.

With newfound prosperity came changes in our nightly dinner conversations. The topic of not having enough money to pay bills was replaced by discussions of charitable causes and helping others. I did not understand the concept of charity and asked a lot of questions about why, who, and how much. They were curious as to why I was so interested. I replied, "If we give all our money away we might have to move back to 37th Street and I don't want to lose my bedroom." They laughed pretty hard at my answer but then got very serious. My parents explained that they had been the recipients of financial help when things were desperate. It was their turn to help others. That conversation served as my introduction to the power of giving and I witnessed the great joy my parents got from sharing their good fortune with those in need. It turned out that some of the same friends who had helped them when they were desperate now needed help themselves, and mom and dad gladly repaid the favor.

For my father's eightieth birthday I sent a letter to some of his friends and clients asking them to acknowledge the occasion. Expecting to receive an assortment of simple birthday cards, I was surprised as stacks of letters started showing up in my mailbox. I knew my father's clients and friends had a deep appreciation for him, but some of their stories and testimonials surprised me. Reading those letters, I realized my father had saved marriages, kept families together, helped create businesses, and advised millionaires. His assistant filled an entire scrapbook with the personal notes and stories.

He was deeply touched when I presented him with the book at his birthday party. It was a very emotional experience. "It is like I am at my funeral and I am hearing what people are saying about me, except I am still alive," he said. "This is pretty amazing!" He told me it was the best birthday present of his life.

My father not only achieved his American Dream, but according to his birthday scrapbook, he helped many others achieve theirs as well.

[
I think back to our family dinners and the discussions that occurred around the dinner table and the impact they had on creating my core values.
]

in the stadium was unbelievable, unlike anything I had ever witnessed. I was so excited that I spent the night in my car, so I could watch the Sunday afternoon game as well. Even though it was over sixty years ago, I remember the Indians winning that game too!"

Another one of Abner's favorite destinations was the race track at Northfield Park. He enjoyed betting on horses and Northfield was conveniently located between Cleveland and Baltic, an easy detour on his journey home. "I really enjoyed my weekend trips to Cleveland," remembers Abner. "In many ways they became life-changing adventures. The brightly-lit big city with thousands of people walking the streets was so strange compared to my life in Baltic." Abner laughed and said there was one other aspect that made each road trip even more exciting: "I never bothered to get a driver's license."

In the eyes of the elders and the community, Abner was following the traditions of the Old Order. He worked the family farm, married, and started a family. But Abner and his wife, Esther, saw their life much differently. They questioned the Order's strict rules and restrictions and decided they wanted to live in a different way. They chose the world Abner had experienced on his weekend excursions.

At the age of twenty-four, Abner and Esther left Baltic and the Order and moved to Canton, Ohio, a city of over 100,000 residents. The move was more difficult and stressful than they anticipated.

Abner had carpentry skills and began working for his brother-in-law building homes. He grew frustrated with this job. After three and a half years, he was only earning two dollars per hour with no sign of a raise. Abner had a family to provide for and felt he was failing.

What Abner calls "fate" intervened in the form of a newspaper advertisement. He was reading a trade journal when an ad for building and selling prefabricated trusses (the wooden supports for roofs) caught his eye. "I knew nothing about trusses or what was involved in owning a business," said Abner, "but something about that advertisement and the potential business opportunity just clicked."

He sent in the money for the information, unsure of what he would get for it. What he received was a workbook explaining what was necessary to start a truss company, a list of the equipment he would need, and blueprints for building trusses. To proceed further required an investment of $8,000, which was a lot of money in 1963. To raise the money, Abner and Esther sold their home, but they still did not have enough. They realized they would have to ask their family for money, something Abner called "unthinkable" at the time. Leaving the Order had not been an aceptable path to take and Abner was not sure how his request would be received. But his

What Abner calls "fate" intervened in the form of a newspaper advertisement.

father agreed to help and loaned Abner the necessary funds for the Stark Truss Company to open its doors.

Abner rented a building and leased the necessary equipment, which turned out to be the easy part of his new business. The hard part was finding buyers for the trusses. The truss workbook neglected to mention that most builders constructed their own trusses and did so on the job. Abner's potential customers asked, "Why would we want to buy trusses from you?" Abner knew if he was going to become successful he would have to answer that question and give the builders a reason to buy from Stark Truss.

Abner and Esther called on their faith in God and prayed to King Solomon for help. The answer they received was that Abner needed to prove to his customers that Stark Truss could make and deliver the trusses more efficiently and less expensively. When I questioned Abner about praying to King Solomon, he replied, "King Solomon was very wise and a great businessman. Why not ask for help from the best?"

Stark Truss got off to a slow start and soon Abner needed additional capital to keep his company afloat. He decided to take on a financial partner but the partnership was fraught with problems and ended quickly. Out of desperation, Abner asked friends and family to invest in his business, but no one was willing to help. "I felt that some of the people who turned me down were waiting for me to go bankrupt," said Abner. "They thought they could grab my business for nothing." His family and friends underestimated how hard Abner would work to save his company. He had determination, drive, and a healthy amount of stubbornness that would never let him succumb to failure.

Stark Truss was a one-man show with Abner building, selling, delivering, invoicing, and collecting customer payments. Eventually sales grew exponentially to the point at which Abner could not keep up. It was a great problem to have, except for one larger problem Abner now had to face. He was a perfectionist and would have to make a leap of faith and trust in employees to perform to his standards. Hiring a workforce gave Abner time to focus on other aspects of the business. He began studying his manufacturing processes and designed new equipment that improved product quality and production speed.

Eventually three of Abner and Esther's children joined the company, freeing up more time for Abner to manage his growing enterprise. The timing was perfect. New home construction hit an all-time high in the early 2000s. Stark Truss expanded to eighteen locations across the country, employed 1,900 people, and produced record sales of over $185,000,000. It was an amazing ride.

The recession of 2007 took its toll on Stark Truss. New home starts crashed and with them went the truss business. Abner and his family made some very difficult decisions, once again guided by their faith. They began the painful process of downsizing. "Every time we encountered a problem, Esther and I would pray for assistance and wait for an answer," said Abner. "It always came." When the final adjustments were completed, ten locations were still operating with approximately 450 employees. "It was hard to start my company," said Abner. "In many ways closing plants was harder. But we had to think about survival."

Esther and Abner have made many important decisions throughout their lives together, but perhaps none were more important than the two they made early in their business career. First, they agreed to always pay their bills before they paid themselves. This decision kept them from spending money they did not have. Second, once Stark Truss became profitable, Esther and Abner agreed to donate ten percent of their annual profits to charity. Little did they know how significant this decision would become or the number of people they would touch with their generosity.

In 1991, the Abner and Esther Yoder Charitable Foundation was established with the goal of supporting Christian-based missions throughout the world. On one of their missionary trips to India, Abner and Esther made the decision to build and fund two orphanages. Their first donations provided housing, education and food for thousands of abandoned children living on the streets of India. Over the last twenty years, Abner and Esther have expanded their charitable reach throughout the world, including the financing of a hospital in Guatemala and an orphanage in Nepal. To date their foundation supports fifty different Christian ministries across the globe.

Abner and Esther have traveled a unique path in their lives, from tilling a farm with a horse and buggy to building a

$100,000,000 company, to traveling the world in support of their charitable foundation.

I asked Abner to sum up his amazing success. He quoted Proverbs 3:5-6: "Trust in the Lord with all your heart and do not lean on your own understanding. In all your ways acknowledge Him, and He will make your paths straight." Then he smiled and said, "Sometimes my path took me straight to Cleveland."

> Abner may have stopped his formal education after the eighth grade but he never stopped learning. He holds patents on a number of inventions that have changed how trusses are built.

5
A STREETWISE
PERSPECTIVE

P egine Echevarria was raised in a tough neighborhood in the Bronx. The streets of her neighborhood were dangerous, filled with criminals, drug dealers, and violence. She could not find refuge in her home; it was filled with dysfunction. One of her sisters had run away and the other died from a heroin overdose—in front of Pegine.

To escape the chaos at home, Pegine turned to the streets and joined an all-girl Puerto Rican gang. The members became her family. She focused her energies on gang life including stealing, intimidation, and causing general mayhem. Belonging to a gang provided street protection from rival gangs and a better chance of surviving the neighborhood violence.

Today Pegine Echevarria is the author of four books, including *Sometimes You Need To… Kick Your Own Butt,* one of my all-time favorite titles. She is one of eight women and the only Latina member inducted into the Motivational Speakers Hall of Fame, which includes such luminaries as Dale Carnegie, Tony Robbins, Jack Canfield, Zig Ziglar, and Wayne Dyer. In addition, Pegine is CEO of Team Pegine, Inc., a company specializing in working with both government and corporate clients to engage, train, and market to diverse communities. Pegine is one impressive woman!

How did she turn her life around from gang member Pegine to award-winning motivational speaker and CEO Pegine? First we need to find out what motivated her to change her life and escape her unstable environment.

Pegine credits three mentors and an author for redirecting her life and putting her on a path toward her American Dream.

The first mentor was a Girl Scout leader named Mrs. B., who formed a troop made up of gang girls. She wanted to help these young women see a different way of life and the possibilities that existed away from the streets. One of Mrs. B.'s exercises was to take the troop to Wall Street and have the scouts interview women as they were walking to their offices. Mrs. B. wanted the girls to question the Wall Street workers about obstacles in their own lives and how they overcame them.

This was a challenging assignment for the scouts. Everyone was in a hurry, moving quickly, and avoiding any type of interaction or distraction. It took some time but Pegine got the hang of walking and talking quickly to keep up. As her communication skills improved, some of the women would stop and talk to her once they understood the reason she was approaching them. It became clear to Pegine that all of the women she interviewed had overcome some sort of adversity in their lives. The stories were many and varied, but all had one important lesson in common: Don't quit, no matter how difficult things are.

Of course, Pegine's gang knew nothing of her Girl Scout activities; she'd have faced ridicule and worse if they did. And this was not her only secret. She loved to read, especially books written by her favorite novelist, Sydney Sheldon. The main characters in these stories were strong female entrepreneurs who achieved financial success. Even though the characters were fictional, they became role models for Pegine. She dreamed of what it would be like to become such an accomplished woman.

When Pegine got expelled from high school for fighting, she was transferred to a new school where the teachers expected more of her than physical toughness. Her new teachers didn't care that she could beat up classmates; they recognized Pegine's potential and challenged her to show her mental toughness and succeed academically. Two teachers in particular, Mrs. H. and Mr. T., became mentors to her.

Mrs. H., who taught Spanish and drama, was not the least bit intimidated by her new student. She confronted Pegine and asked her if she had "real guts," or if she was just all talk and no action. Pegine responded with her tough-girl bravado, only to be floored by what happened next. Mrs. H. offered her the most important drama project of the school year: to write, direct, cast, and produce the high school spring play. This was a very big deal—as well as a great honor. Pegine had never been given this kind of responsibility.

Pegine accepted the drama challenge in spite of feeling Mrs. H. was "mean, nasty, and a royal pain." To this day, Pegine is not sure what really motivated her to agree to take on such a project or why she was so determined not to disappoint Mrs. H. For the first time in her life, people counted on Pegine—and she did not let them down. The project became the focal point of Pegine's life. She wrote and directed a parody of the movie *Grease* and called it *Grime*. The play was a smashing success. The experience gave Pegine a heavy dose of self-confidence and a new set of skills, including project management, set design, leadership, and the ability to manage people, pressure, and deadlines. More importantly, Pegine proved to herself that she could accomplish something difficult and meaningful.

Mr. T. taught her high school English writing class and, according to Pegine, was "a horrible man." He made her angry and rarely had a positive word of encouragement. "He required me to write stories and then had the audacity to give me bad grades for my efforts," recalled Pegine. Yet in the same breath, Pegine mentioned how deeply indebted she was to Mr. T. for all he taught her. Today, she realizes his goal was to teach her how to communicate through the written word. The skills she developed in his class would become the cornerstones of her career as an author.

A positive habit Mr. T. instilled in Pegine was to keep a daily journal. He explained that she was writing for herself; it didn't matter if anyone ever read what she wrote. Pegine said the habit of daily writing became an incredibly powerful tool in both her personal and professional life. "My daily journaling has been instrumental in helping to keep me grounded and to solve problems," said Pegine. Every morning she writes about gratitude, what's going on in her life, and the amazing people who surround her. She has not missed a single day of journaling since the age of sixteen.

It became clear to Pegine that all of the women she interviewed had overcome some sort of adversity in their lives.

When Pegine graduated from high school, college was not an option. The reality was she still lived in the tough Bronx neighborhood and was still a member of a gang. She recognized that her life was a dead end and that she had to break free from her current circumstances if she ever wanted to progress in life. The problem was she didn't know of anywhere she could go and be safe. Pegine had witnessed the beatings other gang members suffered when they tried to leave. She devised a plan; she would leave the country. One night she told her fellow gang members, she'd see them later—and then left.   She never saw any of them again. Pegine spent the next three weeks tucked away at home, avoiding the gang, and planning a move to—Europe!

Although moving abroad sounds extreme to some, Pegine felt the further away from the Bronx and the gang, the safer she would be. She couldn't decide where in Europe she wanted to live, so she made her choice by writing the words England, France, Italy, Germany, and Spain on separate pieces of paper and putting them in a hat. She pulled out Spain. To fund her trip, Pegine said she committed the last crime of her life. She "borrowed" a thousand dollars from her mother to buy a ticket to Madrid. "I was not proud of that," said Pegine, "but I fully intended to repay my mother with interest."

Finding work in Madrid was more difficult than Pegine had anticipated; her inability to speak fluent Spanish was the biggest drawback. After hitting dead end after dead end, Pegine decided to focus her job search on nursery schools, hoping her Spanish was sufficient enough for working with children. She still could not get hired, but she did come up with a great idea. Pegine discovered that Madrid did not have a bilingual nursery school. Following her entrepreneurial instincts and lessons learned from her mentors, Pegine decided to open a school. However, this wasn't an easy undertaking, as she would first need to find seed money. She was introduced to a gentleman, Pedro Bautista, a forty-year-old family man with three children, who wanted to learn English, and when Pegine told him about her business plan and made him a deal to teach him English in exchange for the capital to start her school, he agreed. They became partners in the enterprise.

Within two weeks of opening, the nursery school was fully enrolled and had a waiting list. Pegine and Pedro decided to open two additional locations. Once again, the enrollment exceeded their expectations. The popularity of the schools attracted media attention which, in turn, attracted the attention of a competitor who approached Pegine to explore the possibility of a buyout. He made an offer they could not turn down and Pegine and her partner sold their schools.

After the buyout, Pegine was able to repay her mother. "My mother was understanding and very supportive of my reasons for leaving the country but I was still ashamed of taking her money," said Pegine. "It was a huge burden off my shoulders when I made this right."

Her next entrepreneurial venture was in fashion, a field she entered quite by accident. Women's fashion in Spain was very conservative. Coming from the United States, where the hippie movement was in full force, Pegine wore loose-fitting and colorful peasant dresses. She was often stopped on the street by women who complimented her on how she dressed. She decided to capitalize on what she thought might be an opportunity and began sewing peasant dresses and selling them at a flea market. She sold out at her first market. Pegine knew she was on to a good thing and began a pattern of sewing during the week and selling out every weekend. Her dresses became the fashion rage of the city. A designer from the largest department store in Madrid approached Pegine about buying her patterns and hiring her to teach his staff how to sew her dress designs. They agreed on a price and, once again, she reaped a significant profit from selling a business.

Pegine's entrepreneurial successes did wonderful things for her confidence and self-esteem, but after living abroad for six years she decided it was time to return to the United States and pursue higher education. She enrolled at Hunter College and graduated with a Bachelor of Arts degree.

After college, Pegine took a job as a sales representative for a boat dealer that sold Evinrude Outboard Motors. She was successful in this endeavor and was recognized as a top Evinrude salesperson. Next, Pegine took a job with The Pierre Cardin/Gant Menswear Corporation. They hired her as a receptionist, but quickly recognized her natural talents and moved her into sales. Within two years, Pegine was named national sales manager of the Cardin/Gant Big and Tall Division, which accounted for millions of dollars of sales per year. Her next promotion was to expand their men's clothing line to the Latino market. Not surprisingly, she exceeded the company's sales projections.

After Cardin, Pegine was hired as president of Mother's Network, a women's direct sales catalogue company. As president, her responsibilities included motivating people, fostering leadership skills, and developing teamwork. Pegine was stymied in her new job. She was frustrated with her employees' attitudes and their lack of drive. It bothered her that they lacked the self-motivation to take advantage of business opportunities. Frustrated, she resigned her position as president of Mother's Network and decided to return to school.

Pegine enrolled at Adelphi University to pursue a Masters in Social Work with a focus on leadership. She was on a mission to learn how to motivate people. After graduation she relocated to Jacksonville, Florida, where she opened Team Pegine, Inc. Her new company provides diversity training, leadership coaching for women, and team building. Team Pegine's list of clients include Intel, State Farm, NASA, Harley Davidson, and the United States Army.

For Pegine, her American Dream was to escape the gang and the dangerous environment surrounding her. To accomplish her goal it took three mentors, a novelist, and a bold move to the other side of the world. I asked her for advice on how others can achieve their American Dreams. Her answer: "Sometimes you just have to kick your own butt!"

[I wondered as I wrote Pegine's story what her life would have been like if she had pulled a different card out of the hat.]

6
A FAITH-BASED
PERSPECTIVE

t was Thanksgiving evening and Pat Culpepper was having a difficult time giving thanks for anything. He looked out the window and watched the snow fall, the first flakes of the year in Fenton, Michigan. Pat thought about how he should appreciate such a beautiful sight and how thankful he should feel for having his wife Robin in his life, but at the moment none of it seemed to matter. It felt like the universe was working against him. So many bad things had happened throughout the year that he had lost count. Instead of watching a meaningless football game on television, Pat decided to bundle up and go for a long walk.

On that cold Thanksgiving walk, Pat's thoughts were centered around a meeting with bankers that was scheduled for the next morning. It would be a do-or-die meeting to find out if the bank would loan more money to Pat's business, Expanded Plastics. If they declined, the business—started by his father—would not survive. Pat scoured his brain to come up with anything he could say or do to persuade the bankers to save the company. Nothing really came to mind so Pat did what religious people do; he prayed for help.

Expanded Plastics was in dire financial trouble. There was not enough money to pay the bills or even cover the next payroll. In a final act of desperation, Pat's father had turned the management of the company over to his son. It would take a miracle to save the company, so Pat prayed.

Pat, thirty-two, had worked on and off for the company since he was fourteen. He swept floors, cleaned bathrooms, ran machines, and did whatever he could to help the company. "Expanded Plastics always struggled, largely because of my father's drinking problem," said Pat. "He made some horrible business decisions, one of which was not saving money for the down times. The economic recession of 1991 put the company on life support." It was at that point in time when Pat's father handed him the keys, wished him luck, and walked away. Pat, who lacked any management training, put his heart and soul into saving the company. In spite of his heroic efforts, Expanded Plastics was on the brink of bankruptcy.

What happened to Pat on that Thanksgiving walk was not something that happens to most people on an everyday basis; or maybe it does but we just aren't listening. But Pat was listening.

He was lost in his thoughts when he heard a voice. He looked around to see who was talking to him but there was no one in sight. Pat heard the voice again, this time more loudly and clearly. He knew right away it was not the inner voice he'd become accustomed to hearing lately, reminding him of his failures and looming bankruptcy. No, this voice was different. It was strong, powerful, and immediately commanded his attention.

Pat listened closely as he walked. The voice explained that God had big plans for Pat and his family and that life was going to change in a very positive way. The voice also told Pat that it would be okay if Expanded Plastics disappeared from the face of the earth. In fact, it instructed him to revisit a business idea he had once considered developing. In Pat's own words, "I had a one-way conversation with a Higher Power."

Pat's business idea was the creation of a new product that would revolutionize the aluminum-siding industry. Pat had been exploring a non-traditional approach, combining vinyl siding with an energy-efficient, insulated foam backing. With all of the chaos happening at Expanded Plastics, Pat did not have time to pursue his invention. He simply moved it to the back burner and forgot all about it.

When Pat returned home from his walk, he told Robin about the voice he'd heard and what it had told him. For the first time in a long time, Pat felt energized. "I had a new sense of direction, purpose, and passion," he said. As excited as he was, it was first things first; he still had the morning meeting with the bankers to learn the fate of Expanded Plastics.

Not surprisingly, the meeting went exactly as Pat thought it would—poorly. The family business in Michigan, as well as a sister plant in Dover, Ohio, were forced to file for bankruptcy.

Pat received a first-hand education on dissolving a company. It was an incredibly sad and depressing experience that turned ugly and delivered to Pat an unwelcome and unexpected surprise from the state of Michigan. He learned via registered mail that Expanded Plastics was delinquent on a tax payment of $60,000. His father had misappropriated payroll taxes and used the money to pay other business expenses. The tax delinquency issue grew more daunting when Pat learned that as acting president, he was personally liable for the past-due taxes and penalties. Pat scraped together enough funds from the liquidation of Expanded Plastics to pay the Michigan tax collectors and all remaining creditors.

Not only did Pat find a financial backer, but he also found a friend and mentor.

Now free and clear of Expanded Plastics, Pat focused his attention on developing his new product and forming a company around it. Pat chose the name Progressive Foam and filed patents to protect his invention and process. Next on his agenda was finding a financial backer for the new company. When Pat approached members of the banking community for loans, it quickly became apparent that traditional bank financing was not an option. The institutions required personal collateral to back up the loan, and the bankruptcy of Expanded Plastics had left Pat with virtually zero assets to pledge against any financial obligation.

Pat wasn't sure where to turn when two friends from his church offered a solution. They believed in Pat and loaned him $200,000 on a handshake and his promise to pay them back with interest. Their act of faith and generosity made a deep impression on Pat and Robin. They decided that once Progressive Foam became successful they too were going to help other struggling entrepreneurs. They even named their plan the "Circle of Generosity" and it became the model for their future philanthropy.

Like many new businesses, Progressive Foam struggled in its early years, but Pat persevered, honored his promise to his friends and paid them back in full. Even though sales grew to $2.5 million and the company was no longer in the red, Pat did not have enough capital to grow. He needed a new partner if he was going to expand Progressive Foam into a major company. That partner turned out to be Abner Yoder, whose story appears in chapter 4. Pat interviewed other interested investors but knew that Abner was the right guy. "He was a self-made millionaire and had excellent business instincts," Pat said. Not only did Pat find a financial backer, but he also found a friend and mentor.

With Abner's backing, Progressive Foam moved into a 36,000 square foot building that doubled the company's size and capabilities. Sales grew rapidly as the industry began to warm up to Pat's energy efficient siding. Sales received a further boost when new home construction hit an all-time high. "Just as the voice had predicted on my Thanksgiving walk, my life had changed dramatically," said Pat. "With the help and guidance of Abner, Progressive Foam became a success exceeding all of my dreams and expectations." The Progressive Foam of today occupies 110,000 square feet of space, employees over 135 people, and topped $26,000,000 in sales.

From the first meager earnings of their company, Pat and Robin wanted to honor their commitment to charity. Knowing that you want to help people is one thing; finding them is an entirely different matter. A missionary trip to the Philippines in 1995 introduced the Culpeppers to the idea of funding micro-business loans. The business model fit perfectly with their Circle of Generosity goal of helping entrepreneurs.

The first micro-business they funded was pig farming. Robin and Pat provided the money to buy piglets for ten Philippino families with the understanding that each family would start their own pig farm. Pat smiled and said, "Unfortunately, some people just ate the pigs but most of the recipients followed the business plan and started farms that are still in existence today."

The second micro-business financed by Pat and Robin was a Manilla taxi service with a twist. The Culpeppers purchased the taxis. Drivers included a tax in each fare, which raised money for free medical and dental treatment to impoverished communities throughout the city. The program was a huge success and the Circle of Generosity was officially off and running.

While on another church mission to the Dominican Republic in 2007, the Culpeppers were introduced to an organization called Esperanza International. Esperanza created and managed a micro-business funding program called Bank of Hope that offered an on-site management company. Pat and Robin liked this feature and signed on with Esperanza. They expanded the standard Esperanza agreement to also include loans to men and women entrepreneurs. The Culpeppers increased the initial loan from $125 to $750; Pat and Robin felt the larger loans would give the new businesses a better chance of succeeding.

A critical part of the Esperanza program was how loan recipients were chosen. Pastors who ministered in small, impoverished parishes provided lists of qualified Bank of Hope candidates. After face-to-face meetings with the potential entrepreneurs, the Culpeppers chose five people who would receive their first micro-loans. Although the five businesses were separate entities, there was a clause in the agreement that held each entrepreneur responsible for one another's loans. This created a very close relationship among the start-ups. At the end of the first year Pat and Robin returned to the Dominion Republic for progress reports. Pat was amazed and pleased by the year-end results. Four of the five loans had already been paid back in full.

Meeting with each business owner was rewarding for the Culpeppers, but one man really touched their hearts. When they had first met Caesar a year earlier, he was downtrodden, unemployed, and struggling to feed his family of four. Caesar, who had owned a sewing business, was a broken man, just like his two sewing machines that he could not afford to repair. The Culpeppers' micro-loan allowed Caesar to fix the machines and buy enough material to restart his sewing business. At the same time, a local hotel was searching for a new vendor to sew logo shirts for its gift shop. They hired Caesar on a trial basis. The hotel was impressed with his quality of work and on-time delivery and awarded his new company a long-term contract. At their review, Pat and Robin saw a different man than the one they had met at the first interview. With tears in his eyes, a very proud Caesar reported that not only was he providing for his family, but he had repaid his loan early and hired two employees who were now earning a living and providing for their families.

Caesar was a perfect example of what the Culpeppers were hoping to accomplish when they started the Circle of Generosity. To date, Pat and Robin have expanded their giving to other countries, including the United States, China, Kenya, and Uganda.

So, the next time you feel lost or hopeless, you might consider going for a walk. Perhaps you too will hear an unfamiliar voice full of comfort and guidance. If you do, I suggest you follow Pat's advice, "Pay very close attention. It could change your life and lead you to your American Dream."

[
Faith in a higher power, faith in their fellow man and faith in themselves played a significant role in Pat and Robin's story.
]

7
A FATHER'S PERSPECTIVE

Dear Doug,

Your old man has just finished knocking off all the reports that are due in the office on the first of the month. The first of the month reminds me of some little Buddy's birthday. Actually, you are not what I would call my "Little Buddy" anymore. I guess it's about time I call you my "Big Buddy"!

What I'm trying to tell you is that you have brought a lot of joy to your skinny (!) Dad over the years & I look forward to the weekends with extra special "somethings" as you grow older.

It has been a lot of fun watching you grow up--the legs keep getting longer—the freckles a little larger--the pants keep getting tighter; but then every once in a while we replace some tight pants & you look "in shape" again.

As we both grow older, let us try harder to understand why each of us does what he does, try to live by the Golden Rule, set goals that are not necessarily easy to reach and try to live by those 12 Scout Laws.

Good luck to you today & every day.

Your Dad

Doug Hartley received this letter on his thirteenth birthday. His father, Neil Hartley, could not be home for the occasion. Neil was a traveling salesman for the Wrigley Chewing Gum Company and was on the road when he wrote this letter from his hotel room. Doug keeps the letter as a cherished memory of his father.

Doug and his father had a very close relationship filled with camping trips, Boy Scouts, fishing, and lots of baseball. Neil coached his son's baseball team and recognized Doug's potential as a pitcher. After team practices, he spent extra time with his son working on his pitching technique. He also spent time teaching him the mental side of the game, instructing Doug how to think strategically on the mound, how to size up his opponents, how to stay focused, keep going, and not give up in difficult games. It was not until later in life that Doug realized the instruction he received from his dad was not just about facing batters.

The most enjoyable part of Doug's baseball training was attending professional baseball games with his dad. Their trips to watch the Cleveland Indians were multi-purposed: watching their favorite team, discussing pitching strategy, and spending time together. "My father never missed an opportunity to teach and used sports as a learning experience," said Doug. "He always stressed the importance of teamwork. My dad felt strongly that it was one of the critical keys to becoming successful in sports and life."

Perhaps one of the reasons Neil Hartley sought out so many opportunities to teach Doug life skills was because he knew his time with his son might be short-lived.

Neil had suffered a heart attack at the age of thirty-three, when Doug was a baby. The males in the Hartley family had a history of heart disease and Neil knew there was a strong possibility he would not be around to see Doug grow up. With the odds stacked against him, Neil did everything possible to stay healthy for as long as he could. He was ahead of his time in understanding how important lifestyle was in preserving health. As a boy, Doug witnessed his father's strenuous workouts but was too young to understand why his father pushed himself.

Neil found many ways to impart practical lessons to his son. When Doug asked his father for spending money for a family vacation, Neil told him he would have to earn it. Neil bought Doug a box of candy bars for twenty-five cents each and told him to sell them door-to-door for a dollar apiece. Doug knocked on doors, explained why he was selling candy bars, and sold every single bar the first day. His confidence soared. With a seventy-five cent profit on each candy bar, Doug had plenty of spending money for his vacation.

That same summer Neil bought a lawn mower so Doug could earn money mowing lawns in the neighborhood. The work was difficult but the money was good. Neil wanted to teach Doug that hard work would generate rewards. This important lesson was a lot to absorb for a ten-year-old boy, but it created a great foundation for Doug's future.

Doug's lessons continued during his school vacations. Whenever possible, Neil would take his son to work with him. They called on accounts together and Doug would listen to his father's sales pitches. "This one-on-one time was fantastic," remembers Doug. "We talked sales, why customers bought Wrigley gum, how he earned their business and how he kept their business. I was soaking up my father's wisdom."

Shortly after Doug's thirteenth birthday, Neil, in failing health, entered the intensive care unit of the Cleveland Clinic. He'd been consulting with the clinic's heart specialists and was a candidate for a newly developed heart procedure. Neil was placed on a list of candidates to undergo one of the first bypass surgeries performed at the clinic.

Doug and his mother spent what time they could with Neil at the hospital, but visitation rules were strict. One visit will always be etched in Doug's mind. He and his mother were at his dad's bedside when a nurse entered the room and asked them to leave. Neil asked if it would be okay for his son to stay longer but the nurse said, "No." A heated argument ensued, and Doug's mother left the room as Doug was finally permitted to stay. Neil told his young son it was time to have a man-to-man talk; he told Doug he would have to be "the man of the house" going forward. "You will mow the grass; fix whatever you can in the house; earn your own spending money; and always treat your grandmother, mother and sister with respect," instructed Neil. Those were the last words Doug heard from his father and he has never forgotten them. Neil passed away shortly after that hospital conversation.

Doug went into shock. He knew his father was not well but he'd never really grasped the severity of his heart condition. Now he had to face the finality of his father's death; the realization that he would never see or talk to his dad again was devastating.

Doug had a difficult time resuming his old activities. He found a new interest in music, specifically the drums. He joined the marching band at Cuyahoga Falls High School where he fell under the influence of band director, Robert Felbush, a no-nonsense type of guy with a personality and manner similar to Neil. He became Doug's mentor. Felbush brought stability and purpose back into Doug's life. Doug doubts that his band director ever realized just how important he was to him during this critical time in his life.

Doug remembered one of his dad's lessons: Don't give up.

In his junior year Doug tried out for the Goldtones, the high school jazz band. He didn't make the cut, though, and was very discouraged. But Doug remembered one of his dad's lessons: "Don't give up." Doug practiced for a whole year with one goal in mind: to become the drummer for the Goldtones. The odds of joining the elite group were stacked against him as seniors rarely beat out juniors, but Doug elected to ignore the odds, kept practicing, and earned the coveted spot in the jazz band. Doug felt his achievement was a tribute to his father.

Throughout high school, Doug played drums in various rock bands. He was invited to audition for a new band that was forming in Kent, Ohio, and nailed his tryout. They hired him on the spot. The band developed a large following and secured bookings throughout Ohio. Doug thought his future was set; he had never made so much money and he was having a blast doing what he loved. Unfortunately, when one of the key members of the band had to leave because of a family crisis, the band lost all momentum and soon dissolved. By this time, Doug had married and his wife, Irene, was pregnant with their first child. The lack of stability in the world of music provided a wakeup call. It was time for him to get a "real" job.

Doug's first nine-to-five job was in the mail room at B. F. Goodrich in Akron, Ohio. The pay was not great but the job provided a steady income. It was not long before Doug was promoted to the accounting department. Doug was happy with his promotion, but unhappy in accounting. He wanted to move into sales, but Goodrich had a policy that required a college degree in order to be considered for a sales position. Although Doug had attended classes at Akron University, he'd never graduated. Eventually, he left Goodrich and took a job with the Goldsmith and Eggleton Company, an Akron-based rubber polymer dealer and preprocessor of scrap synthetic rubber. The opportunity to advance in the company did not require a college degree.

It took one year before Doug was promoted to a sales position brokering rubber to the tire industry. Like his father, Doug was a natural at sales and excelled in the position. As a reward for his success, he was transferred to the company's Chicago office, where they needed help in their sales department.

The Chicago move was significant for Doug on both a personal and business level. The position came with a substantial pay raise and provided the introduction to his next mentor, Marvin Weintraub. Doug and Marvin spent countless hours together and became very close. He was invited into the Weintraub home for holiday celebrations and became a surrogate member of the family. Doug loved spending time with his new boss. Under Marvin's tutelage, Doug's responsibilities grew from regional sales manager to national sales manager, then eventually to vice president of worldwide sales. Doug never dreamed he would have such a prestigious title or that he would earn such a good living. "I thought I was set for life and would finish my career at Goldsmith and Eggleston," said Doug. But everything changed when his son presented him with a proposition he could not refuse.

In 2002, Doug's son, Rick, approached him about starting a new company together. Doug, who had often thought about how amazing it would have been to have worked with his own father, could not pass up the chance to work with his son. He left Goldsmith and Eggleston and used his industry experience to open Portage Precision Polymers Inc., a company that mixes and compounds rubber. The company started with six employees, including Doug, Irene, and Rick. Starting a business from scratch meant no paychecks. "We ate a lot of peanut butter and jelly sandwiches," said Doug.

During the early days of the company Doug faced another tragedy. Irene was diagnosed with cancer. She fought a courageous battle but ultimately succumbed to the disease. Irene's death put Doug in an emotional tailspin reminiscent of when he lost his father. This time, he said, it was more difficult to recover. "We met at age twenty and it was love at first sight," said Doug. "Irene was my wife, best friend, and mother of our two children." In spite of Irene's death or perhaps because of it, Doug focused even more of his time and energy into building his new company. Twelve years after opening the doors, Portage Precision Polymers had expanded to a second location, had grown to eighty employees, and achieved record sales.

A few years after Irene's death, Doug met Shelby Reeves. The two found they had many things in common, including losing spouses to cancer and owning businesses. Shelby had inherited her husband's failing business, which she succeeded in turning around. They married in 2007 and Shelby became a trusted business advisor for Doug, especially when Hexpol Compounding, the largest rubber compounder in the world, came calling to buy Portage Precision Polymers.

After a series of negotiations and with Shelby's guidance and advice, Doug accepted the Hexpol offer. "It was an extremely difficult decision," said Doug. "Shelby was a wonderful sounding board and helped me work through the pros and cons of the sale.

Sometimes you really need a woman's perspective to make sense out of stuff." Part of the agreement included an employment contract that allows Doug to stay involved with the company he and his son founded.

Doug has read and reread his father's letter so many times the paper is tattered and the ink has faded. But the advice has never grown old; his father's words and lessons have guided Doug throughout his life. Neil Hartley would be very proud.

[
In many ways his father's letter provided a road map and inspiration for Doug's life. Without question it is one of his most cherished possessions.
]

8
A SURVIVOR'S PERSPECTIVE

Thaddeus Stabholz was the doctor for my high school basketball team. As one of the smallest guys on the team, I was constantly visiting him to get my battered body put back together. Dr. Ted, as he wished to be called, always greeted me with a huge smile, spoke English with a heavy foreign accent, and made the time to see me even though his waiting room was jam-packed with patients. He refused to accept any money for my visits. Every time I would attempt to pay, the office manager would smile and say: "No charge."

After high school I didn't have any contact with Dr. Stabholz until I entered the financial services business and he became a client. It was during our business relationship that we became friends and I learned about his remarkable and inspiring life.

Thaddeus Stabholz was born in Warsaw, Poland, in 1916. He grew up in an upper-middle-class family and—I am quite sure—spent little, if any, time thinking about the American Dream or the United States, for that matter. His father was a prominent physician and chief of staff of the Jewish Hospital in Warsaw. Thaddeus followed in his father's footsteps and attended medical school until the German army invaded Poland. It was 1939 and life would never be the same for the Stabholz family.

By 1940, the Nazis had rounded up the Jewish community and forced them to live in a tiny area of the city that became known as the Warsaw Ghetto, which was separated from the rest of the city with barbed wire. The overcrowded living conditions were horrible. There was a severe shortage of medicines and little food to go around. The Jews were promised by the Nazis that the ghetto situation was temporary and they would be resettled elsewhere. Thaddeus continued his medical training with night classes at a make-shift underground medical school taught by ghetto doctors. During the day, he worked twelve-hour shifts in the ghetto hospital. In 1942, the Nazis began deporting the Jews to death camps. When it became apparent that resettlement was a lie, the Jews of the Warsaw Ghetto, including Thaddeus Stabholz, began forming resistance units armed with smuggled guns and knives.

The Nazis responded with a full-on attack on the ghetto on April 19, 1943. A small number of poorly armed and untrained Jews waged a hopeless fight against a well-equipped army of several thousand soldiers. The battle, which became known as the

Warsaw Ghetto Uprising, lasted four days before the German soldiers gained control and the freedom fighters surrendered. The surviving Jews were captured and either murdered or placed in concentration camps. Thaddeus was sent to the Treblinka extermination camp.

The day of his capture was the beginning of Dr. Stabholz's journey through hell. His tour included imprisonment in seven different concentration camps: Warsaw Ghetto, Treblinka, Maidanek, Auschwitz II, Sachaenhausen, Dachau XI, and Dachau IV. Few people managed to live through the starvation, torture, and brutality of one camp—let alone seven.

Dachau IV was the last camp for Dr. Stabholz. This death camp was liberated by American soldiers in April 1945 and he was rescued from two years of captivity and brutality. He weighed seventy pounds and was near death. He was taken to a United States military hospital in Europe where he stayed for more than six months. It was a slow process regaining his health after years of malnutrition.

Dr. Stabholz saw his move to the United States as an opportunity to start a new chapter in his life.

Physically Dr. Stabholz had survived the camps, but mentally he was still a prisoner. He began to suffer from a recurring nightmare. His dream took him back to the torture and slaughter he had witnessed in the camps. Gas chambers, beatings, and the murder of innocent people and friends tormented his nights. He would wake up in a cold sweat, afraid to go back to sleep. "It was like being tortured over and over again every time I closed my eyes," explained Dr. Stabholz. "There was a haunting question that plagued me. Why had I been spared when so many around me had lost their lives?"

At the suggestion of a nurse, Dr. Stabholz began writing a journal about the camps and his rescue. "Night and day I wrote like a man possessed," he said. The writing was cathartic and helped put an end to his torturous dreams. His journal eventually became the book *Seven Hells*, which was published in March 1990 by the Holocaust Library.

In addition to chronicling and describing the horrors of his captivity, Dr. Stabholz wrote about his will to live and how he used his medical training to help his fellow prisoners. He also wrote about chance, luck, and intuition—all of which he felt played a part in his survival.

In one instance, prison guards ordered Thaddeus to go with a group of fellow prisoners to eat. Starvation was the norm in the camps and being offered food was rare. Dr. Stabholz was ready to follow the guards when he said he heard the voice of his deceased mother, who had perished in one of the prison camps, telling him not to go. That decision to listen to the voice turned out to be the difference between life and death. The prisoners who followed the Nazi guards were shot. "Was it a voice, my intuition, or was I just lucky? I do not know," observed Dr. Stabholz.

Another example of Dr. Stabholz's "luck" occurred while he was imprisoned at Auschwitz II. Auschwitz was known for its brutal experiments conducted on prisoners. This particular experiment forced young males to immerse one foot into a bucket of boiling water while at the same time immersing the other foot into a bucket of freezing water. The Nazi "doctors" wanted to observe what happened to the men. After the so-called experiment, the prisoner was shot. Dr. Stabholz was the next in line but as he approached the buckets, the sound of airplanes and air raid sirens interrupted the experiment. It was the Allied Forces flying over the prison camp. His Nazi torturers ran for cover and left him standing alone in the room. "The timing of the Allied attack was truly a miracle," he remembered.

During his six-month recovery, Dr. Stabholz had plenty of time to think about his future and decided he would not return to Poland. Instead, he decided to move to the United States where a cousin lived. Thaddeus also wanted to continue pursuit of his medical degree. With a letter of recommendation from a friend, Dr. Stabholz applied and was accepted to the medical school at the University of Vermont in Burlington.

Dr. Stabholz saw his move to the United States as an opportunity to start a new chapter in his life. But before he could begin, there were two major obstacles to overcome. One, he had very little money; his family had lost everything in the war. Two, he spoke very little English. Medical school would be difficult enough, but taking and passing courses in a language he did not know very well would be next to impossible. He decided to give himself a year to learn the language and become familiar with the US culture before starting classes. The university helped him with his finances by giving him a job as a janitor. Thaddeus attended classes during the day and worked at his job during the night. The odds of Thaddeus finishing medical school and passing the medical boards were not in his favor, but then again, this was a man who had survived seven death camps. "As difficult as it was, it was nothing compared to what I had done to survive," he said.

Dr. Stabholz graduated from medical school in 1955 and moved to the small town of Fremont, Ohio, to begin his first job as a physician. That job turned out to be a stepping stone to a position in Canton, Ohio, where a local hospital offered him a job as an emergency room physician. After a few years, Dr. Stabholz took another very large step forward and opened his own practice. It had always been a goal to have his own office, and he was very proud of his achievement.

Dr. Stabholz was a classy man. He was always dressed in suits and ties, had a wonderful sense of humor, loved his family, and was proud to live in America. His charisma and smile could take over a room. These qualities helped him build a very successful medical practice and also served him well in later years when he traveled the country telling his story of Holocaust survival. As painful as his memories were, he felt compelled to educate as many people as he could about the Holocaust, especially high school students.

As Dr. Stabholz's financial advisor, I spoke with him often about money. Dr. Stabholz appreciated the money he earned from his practice and the lifestyle it provided for his family, but money was not his motivation. "I never let money get in the way of my true mission in life, to heal people," he said. As his mission clearly stated, Dr. Stabholz saw patients regardless of their ability to pay for his services. With a broad smile and strong Polish accent, he told many patients they could pay him when they could afford it. These patients appreciated Dr. Stabholz, which was clear on many of my visits to his office where I'd find baskets of homemade muffins and home-grown vegetables covering the tables in his waiting room.

During one of our meetings, I asked Dr. Stabholz about his Holocaust experience and how he survived the verbal and physical abuse in the concentration camps. He explained, "I tried to maintain a positive mental attitude, even though I was surrounded by deplorable conditions, starvation, and death. I concentrated on helping my fellow prisoners with their health problems."

Dr. Stabholz also said humor was a key component to his survival. He told me the prisoners were quite creative with their gallows humor. They held beauty contests, voting on the skinniest bodies and awarding mock prizes. They made fun of the paltry meals, pretending the food was gourmet and served on fine silk tablecloths and the finest china. "We played a game called hide the potato," said Dr. Stabholz. "If you were lucky enough to find a piece of potato in your watered-down vegetable soup, you would win the imaginary prize." He explained that laughter helped alleviate the tension and fear. In some way, laughing gave the prisoners hope for the future.

The United States welcomed Thaddeus Stabholz and other survivors of the Holocaust and offered them asylum and opportunity. Dr. Stabholz appreciated living in America for many reasons, but none was quite as important as the one he referenced in the dedication of his book, *Seven Hells*.

"To my daughters Peggy and Betty with the hope that they may always live in freedom."

[
On days when nothing is going right I sometimes think about the horrors that Dr. Stabholz lived through. My problems become microscopic by comparison.
]

9
A CHALLENGED PERSPECTIVE

Florence Siegel was perplexed. By most measures, her son Andy was a normal kid. He was funny, smart, and had lots of friends. He loved sports and didn't get into much trouble. But at school, Andy was not normal. According to his teachers Andy struggled in the classroom. Those difficulties were reflected in his report cards; he carried a C average. Mrs. Siegel knew her son was not lazy. Every night he spent hours working on his homework, but his grades never seemed to improve. Something was clearly amiss. Eventually, Mrs. Siegel was informed by the school that her son had a learning disability. This news did not surprise her. The question was, how could she help her son?

Andy grew up in a modest home in Cleveland, Ohio, and attended public school. In spite of his lackluster grades, Mrs.

Siegel always believed there was something truly special about her son. She was determined to do everything in her power to provide him an opportunity to succeed. The Siegels were a working class family. They did not have excess money to spend, but education was extremely important. Andy's mother hired tutors to help with his studies. It was a sacrifice and a gamble, but one she was willing to make because she was sure the investment in her son's education would be a wise choice, and the right choice.

In spite of his academic problems, Andy was positive about his future. His goal was to graduate from high school, continue on to college, and become a businessman. The roadblocks to achieving his goals were often overwhelming, but Andy persevered.

Graduating from high school required Andy to receive a passing grade in French. As difficult as regular classes were for him, foreign languages were next to impossible. He had already failed Spanish and Hebrew and was currently failing his French class. Andy set up a meeting with his guidance counselor to see if there was any way around the language requirement. He found out, much to his dismay, that there were no exceptions. He had to achieve a passing grade on the French final exam to receive his high school diploma.

A school advisor encouraged Andy to forget about college and instead find a technical school that would accept him. That suggestion did not sit well with Andy or his mother, who saw his future much differently. But Andy's positive attitude and refusal to quit could only go so far, he still had to pass French. Once again Mrs. Siegel played a significant part in her son's life. Andy's French teacher happened to be a neighbor and close friend of his mother. Somehow, with perhaps a little help from a friend, Andy miraculously passed his French final and graduated with his class.

After receiving his diploma, Andy began a national search to find a college that did not have a foreign language requirement; he knew his learning disability would prevent him from passing a college level foreign language class. His research uncovered two universities that fit the bill, one located in Hawaii and the other in Florida. Andy opted for the University of Tampa because it was less expensive than the other.

Florence Siegel had to take out loans to pay her son's college tuition. Aware that his mother had made this sacrifice added an extra level of stress and responsibility on Andy. He could not disappoint his mother. Andy chose to major in accounting because math was his best subject and required very little reading. Still, in order to receive passing grades, Andy said he had to study all the time, including weekends when his friends were out having fun. He worked hard and remained focused on his ultimate goal of becoming a college graduate. His strategy proved successful; Andy earned a Bachelor of Science degree in Accounting and Business Management with a minor in Economics.

After graduation, Andy returned to Cleveland and began a traditional life path. He started his first job as an accountant and met a girl whom he married. After five years of what he thought was a normal life, that path took several unexpected turns. The marriage ended in divorce and he quit his accounting job.

Andy found a new position as the comptroller for Executone of Cleveland, which introduced him to the dynamic telephone and communications industry. Al Smith, owner of the Cleveland Executone franchise, became a close friend and business mentor. Andy spent as much time as possible with Smith learning the many aspects of managing a business. When Smith was offered an expansion opportunity in Albuquerque, New Mexico, he asked Andy to manage it. He accepted the offer and, without knowing a soul, moved to Albuquerque to start a new life and a new business.

While his skeptical competitors took a wait-and-see attitude, Andy saw an amazing opportunity.

The year was 1983 and the telephone industry was going through a government-imposed deregulation. Much of what Andy had learned in the Cleveland operation was no longer valid. Deregulation changed virtually every aspect of the industry and made it difficult for a new company to survive.

With the telephone industry in total upheaval, Andy began to think about other ways he could earn a living. Ironically, an idea presented itself when Andy began searching for a company to process Executone's weekly payroll. In Cleveland, Andy had utilized a payroll service, but was unable to find such a company in New Mexico. Andy saw this uncharted territory as a business opportunity and began learning everything he could about the payroll business. After studying the industry, he decided to open his own payroll company with the goal of becoming the number one payroll service in New Mexico.

Next on the agenda was gathering the money to start his company. With few assets and no collateral, securing a loan was a difficult task. But Andy did not give up easily; he was used to difficult tasks. After many rejections he finally convinced a loan officer from a local bank to finance his new business. The banker loaned him $6,000 to buy the state-of-the-art computer equipment to get Andy going; in 1985, that meant floppy discs and a dot matrix printer. In June of that year, Andy launched his American Dream, Payday Inc.

Payday started as a one-man operation as Andy sold his payroll services by day and processed what he sold at night. In his first year of operation, Andy had secured thirty customers which, on the surface, was a very impressive number. Below the surface, however, was an entirely different picture. Andy had created a huge problem. He could not service any more businesses; his time was maxed out and he needed help. The obvious solution was to hire an employee, but that was problematic because to hire someone he'd need to be able to pay them, and Payday was barely breaking even. This scenario is a common problem with start-up companies.

Always thinking, Andy came up with a very creative solution to his dilemma. He offered his girlfriend, Sylvana, the job. He explained the company lacked the funds to pay her, but the fringe benefit package would be very good. Upon examination, Sylvana determined there weren't any fringe benefits for her role, so she made a counter offer. She would accept Andy's offer with one significant change: that they get married. Andy made a very wise decision when he accepted Sylvana's new contract language; they worked together as a great team for thirty-five years.

After the initial $6,000 loan, Andy financed Payday through personal credit cards, often maxing out his available credit just to keep the company afloat. A typical Saturday night was spent hand writing letters to potential customers explaining Payday's merits. On Monday morning, they would mail the letters and Andy would spend the rest of the week following up each letter with a personal visit. "We considered ourselves successful if, at the end of the week, we had made enough money for both food and the next week's postage," said Andy.

After eight years of struggling to keep Payday Inc. above water, Andy and Sylvana caught a break. A computer company developed the first custom software package tailor-made for the payroll industry. This was the breakthrough that Andy had been waiting for. While his skeptical competitors took a wait-and-see attitude, Andy saw amazing opportunity. The new software would enable Payday to process payroll anywhere throughout the country.

Andy cleaned out their bank account, purchased the new software, and started an aggressive national marketing campaign; this gamble paid off handsomely. With new software and the confidence that his company could perform and deliver a superior service, Andy began closing sale after sale, including securing the payroll account for a home health care agency with locations across the United States. Today Payday, Inc., located in Albuquerque New Mexico, employs forty people and services 1,900 clients throughout the country.

Payday's success has given Andy a platform to tell his story of trials, tribulations, and ultimate success. He talks about his own disability which, at age thirty, was diagnosed as the reading disorder dyslexia. Andy's favorite audience is inner-city children. When he speaks to them he explains how important it is for them to establish good habits, set goals, and—most importantly—never give up. He tells them that everyone encounters adversity in their lives but that they can overcome anything, just like he did. Andy also stresses the importance of mentors, like Al Smith, and role models, like his mother.

Florence Siegel believed in her son with her heart, soul, and checkbook. Andy acknowledges the critical role his mother's love and support played in his life. "She always believed in me, even when others told her it was a waste of time and money," he said. "My success might not have happened without my mother's faith and unwavering belief in my abilities."

"And," he added, "It didn't hurt that one of my mother's best friends was my French teacher!"

[
Andy overcame roadblocks with hard work, an ability to see opportunity and a willingness to take chances.
]

10
A POLITICAL
PERSPECTIVE

Y our driver pulls up to the security gates of the White House and you wait patiently while the guards inspect your credentials and the vehicle. After they finish, the gates open and you are admitted to the grounds. After parking at the West Wing, you attend a meeting in the Oval Office. At the appointed time, you head across the South Lawn and board Marine One. You have never been in a helicopter so you are totally focused on settling aboard safely. After a moment you look up to discover you are sitting face-to-face across from arguably the most powerful person on the planet, George W. Bush, President of the United States of America. You are Janet Weir Creighton and you have an amazing story, an American Dream come true.

Janet grew up in Canton, Ohio, graduated from high school, and began her pursuit of a college degree at Ohio University in

Athens, Ohio. Her future was filled with endless possibilities and unlimited opportunities. The world was hers to be had. That feeling quickly vanished, however, when a visit to a physician confirmed that she was pregnant. With little recourse, Janet dropped out of Ohio University and returned home, where the conversation she had to have with her parents was not pleasant. Their emotions moved from devastation to disappointment and everywhere in between.

At age eighteen, Janet knew her life was not on the course she had planned. Ultimately, she married the father of her child and became a full-time mother, something she was totally unprepared for and knew nothing about. Another child joined the family before her marriage ended.

By age twenty-six, Janet was divorced and raising two young children on her own; she had to earn a living. She found a part-time office position with Canton City Schools that paid a salary of $6,000 per year. It wasn't enough money to make ends meet, but it was a start.

What Janet lacked in work experience, she made up for in personality. "I was outgoing and on a mission to improve my life," says Janet, "but I really had no idea how that was going to happen. Then a very unlikely door opened and I was introduced to the world of politics."

Someone she knew through her job at the school invited her to attend a political meeting for a new and virtually unknown candidate named Jerry Patrick. He was running for a position in local government and was looking for volunteers to help with his campaign. Janet said she decided to attend the meeting for two reasons. "I was always intrigued by politics and how the system worked and I saw it as a kind of social event, a night out of the house."

Janet made three observations that evening. First, she was the only woman in attendance. Second, the meeting had no agenda and no structure. Third, no one was writing anything down. In Janet's eyes, the meeting was dysfunctional. People made commitments and promises to work for the campaign, but no one kept track of what was being said or who was saying it. Janet volunteered to act as secretary and began taking minutes and recording the names of those who had committed to help.

At the second meeting, Janet brought accountability to the campaign when she pulled out her minutes from the first meeting and reminded the others of their assignments and promises. Patrick was duly impressed, and at the meeting's conclusion he approached Janet and asked her to become his campaign manager. She accepted his offer, a decision that would alter the course of her life.

Patrick lost that election, but with Janet running his next campaign the following year, he won a seat as a Stark County Commissioner. Patrick was now in a position of power and his first official action was to create a countywide Complaint Department. Not surprisingly, he recommended that Janet be appointed the manager of the new department. His fellow commissioners approved Janet's hire and she accepted the appointment and the healthy salary that accompanied the position. Janet was fully aware that the newly-created department was a payback, a political thank-you for helping Patrick win his election.

The salary increase that came with her title was a great benefit, but the true value of the job was the education Janet received from managing the department. As complaints poured in, Janet needed to learn how to get things done and—quickly. First and foremost was to determine who to call. Janet discovered that every department had their "movers and shakers" who got things done. After she identified the key players, her top priority was to get to know them. "I told them that we were on the same team and that I would help them with their problems if they helped me solve mine," explained Janet. She was true to her word and gained respect and credibility among the county departments.

Janet recognized that the county departments, although dependent on each other, lacked communication. She became the conduit among the different departments. "When bad stuff happened in the county," said Janet, "I was the go-to person to get things fixed." She excelled at helping her fellow county workers get what they needed to get their jobs done. "I did what I said I would and made sure that I got it done when I said I would," she said. "My reputation was spreading in a good way. I made a lot of friends throughout the county for just doing what I was hired to do."

In addition to the county position, Janet was recruited by a friend to take a part-time job selling cosmetics door-to-door for Avon Products. It turned out she was a natural-born sales star. It didn't take long for Avon to offer Janet a full-time management position to recruit and train sales women in the Canton area. She accepted the job, which meant she had to give up her government position. Janet excelled in her new position. She hired and managed a 330-woman sales force for Avon. Her sales territory ranked in the top ten percent in the country, and Janet's annual income hit an all-time high.

The friend who had convinced Janet to join Avon left for a job with Time Warner Cable and wanted Janet to join her. She made Janet an offer that came with a substantial pay raise and multiple perks, including a company car and a generous expense account. Janet left Avon for Time Warner. Unfortunately, and without warning, Janet's world soon came crashing down. The cable company eliminated her department and her job. Janet was at a crossroads in her life and was devastated by the suddenness of the company's decision and her loss of income. "The positive side of the situation was that it forced me to take a hard look at my life, both past and future, and determine what my next move would be," she said.

Janet realized she had thoroughly enjoyed working in politics. She scanned the local political scene and decided to run for the vacant Stark County Recorder seat. Once again she was the beneficiary of her friendship with Jerry Patrick. He and the other commissioners appointed Janet to fill the vacancy until the Republican Party chose a permanent replacement for the remaining term.

When Janet informed the Party officials that she had taken out a petition to run in the primary election for the office of County Recorder, she was told the Party had other plans. The chairman asked her to withdraw her petition because they were backing a male candidate for the office. If Janet ran, she would be running without the Republican Party's support.

Janet did not take rejection lightly. She refused to withdraw and waged her own primary campaign. She formed an election committee that developed a strategy, creating confusion on the primary ballot for the Republican-backed candidate. One of Janet's trusted advisors recruited an additional candidate to enter the primary; the new candidate had the same last name as the Party choice. The aggressive strategy worked beautifully. The two same-named candidates split the vote and Janet cruised to victory. The local Republican Party officials went ballistic and refused to talk to Janet for nine months. Reluctantly, they backed her campaign in the general election and Janet won by 3,000 votes.

The President responded by saying, "That's OK Mayor. You will be fine."

Shortly after winning, Janet found herself in the middle of a countywide budget crisis. To help balance the budget, the county commissioners asked each department head to eliminate one of their employees. Janet took their suggestion under advisement but devised her own plan to reduce expenses. She refused a pay raise that was being instituted for elected officials and, instead, used that money to pay her employee's salary and save the position. The story made national news when broadcasting legend, Paul Harvey, told his audience about Janet's creative solution on his syndicated radio show.

The powers in the Stark County Republican Party recognized that Janet was a force to be reckoned with and wisely decided to support her in any future races. In fact, they asked Janet to run for Stark County Auditor in 1991 and she won by an impressive 15,000 votes.

Janet had held the position for twelve years when the Republican Party, now a staunch supporter, approached her to run for mayor. She knew it would be a hard-fought campaign against a strong and well-respected Democratic opponent. There were many hurdles to overcome, but perhaps none larger than her gender. Would the city of Canton elect a female mayor? After much thought, Janet accepted the nomination, ran a strong campaign, and won the mayor's race in a close election. Janet thrived in the mayoral spotlight and was an excellent ambassador for all things Canton.

One of her first official duties was to attend the Presidential Christmas Party at the White House. "It was a bit overwhelming to be in the company of President George W. Bush and his

White House staff," said Janet. "What surprised me was how much they knew about me and my mayoral race. I was surprised by how much attention was paid to my victory."

For Janet, it was hard to imagine how life could be any better. She had become the first female mayor in her hometown and she had met the President of the United States. Under her watch, the city was doing better than it had been before she took office. She thought her re-election was a forgone conclusion.

Unfortunately for Janet, there was a significant shift of political momentum running through the country. Even though Janet was very popular, the Republican Party was not. President Bush's approval rating was in serious decline. The anti-Republican trends found their way to Canton and Janet lost her race. "My opponent out-worked me and that was something that had never happened before," she said. "I was stunned and angry, but I never shed a tear."

Even though Janet had lost her bid for re-election and felt she had let the Republican Party down, she chose to accept another invitation to the annual White House Christmas party. When Janet was greeted by President Bush, she apologized for losing the election. The President responded by saying, "That's OK, Mayor. You will be fine." Janet had no idea what the President meant by his comments, but soon found out when she was asked to return to Washington. It was the final year of Bush's presidency and the White House had a job vacancy that fit Janet's skill set.

Janet was nervous about her interview, as she was competing with three other applicants. The vetting process was extremely thorough and the job required a high level of security clearance. Janet knew the security aspect would not be a problem, but she did have one major concern about her past. She was worried she would be disqualified because she did not have a college degree. During the first interview, Janet addressed her concern and was told that college would not be a deal breaker if she was otherwise qualified.

Janet prevailed and was appointed as the Deputy Assistant to the President of the United States and Director of the White House Office of Intergovernmental Affairs. Her office, staffed by eleven employees, was the first contact point for over 500,000 government officials, including governors, mayors, and state and local politicians. The office also serviced the five US territories and over five hundred Native American tribes. If a natural disaster, such as a hurricane, flood, or tornado, occurred in one of these domains, they called the Office of Intergovernmental Affairs for assistance.

It took some time for Janet to get a clear understanding of how her department worked. In many ways it was similar to her first political appointment at the County Complaint Department, except on a much grander scale. Once again, Janet recognized that it was not the head of the departments that got things done; it was the people who worked for them that really made things happen. Janet referred to these talented people as operatives and there was a network of them that stretched across the country. Janet went back to basics and focused on helping the operatives solve their problems. "I used the same formula of doing what I said I would do and getting it done when I said I would," said Janet, "The only difference was that this time it was on a national level."

Janet spent a year in Washington. She had power, influence, and incredible experiences. Janet's responsibilities included visiting US territories and military bases around the globe. Her means of transportation was Air Force One. She attended state dinners for visiting dignitaries, and had her own car, driver, and parking space at the White House. Janet said, "It was amazing how fast the year went before the President's term ended. The next day it was all over. It disappeared overnight. It was a massive let-down to be so involved and then, nothing."

Janet was once again unemployed with no ideas of what she would do next. But Janet is a survivor and, after taking some time off, she returned to familiar territory. She examined the local political scene and decided to run for the office of Stark County Commissioner. Janet won the election and still holds the position today. Ironically, it is the same position she helped Jerry Patrick win forty years prior.

Throughout the process of interviewing Janet for my book, we had a number of discussions regarding the existence and relevancy of the American Dream. In one of our conversations Janet said, "I have achieved my American Dream. It was not handed to me. I started at the bottom; there were trials and tribulations; but I worked hard to overcome my setbacks. I am both proud and humbled by what I have accomplished. And, by the way, I am not done yet."

[
Janet applied the lessons she learned in her first political job in the county complaint department to her Washington DC position.
]

11
A KID'S
PERSPECTIVE

Confident and in control describe thirty-four-year-old entrepreneur Todd Brook. He learned at a young age what it took to get what he wanted and he has never forgotten those lessons.

Todd was twelve years old when he asked his father to buy him a computer. His father declined but offered Todd a counter proposal: he would match every dollar that Todd earned. They shook hands and Todd went to work doing odd jobs at his house and for the neighbors. "I wanted a computer and I was going to earn it, no questions asked," said Todd.

Although his father made a generous offer, it required a serious commitment on Todd's part. "Computers were expensive in 1992 and I had to work long and hard to earn enough money to pay for my half," said Todd. The father/son deal evolved into much more than just earning money to buy a computer. It taught Todd lessons that have stayed with him throughout his life: goal setting, working with a purpose, finishing what you start, and perseverance. "I managed to save a lot of money despite the temptation of spending it on my short-term wants," he said. For a twelve-year-old kid the responsibility of money management was a lot to handle. Perhaps the most significant lesson occurred on the day Todd walked out of the store with his new computer. "Achieving my goal was an awesome feeling I will never forget," he said. "I was excited and proud of my accomplishment!" Todd became familiar with all aspects of his computer, including taking it apart and repairing it when it wasn't working. "You could say I taught myself the intimate details of the home computer," said Todd.

The following year Todd and one of his friends walked into a retail computer game store at a local mall. They parked themselves in front of a computer and began playing a new game demo. The store owner paid zero attention to them. He was in the middle of a deep discussion with one of his employees as they became mesmerized by the computer screen.

When the owner of the store slapped the counter uttering words of frustration, Todd went over and asked him what was wrong. The owner was obviously upset but, for some reason, took the time to share his computer problem with the young teen. "I listened and told him how to fix it," said Todd, "and then went back to my game."

A couple of minutes later the owner approached Todd, thanked him, and asked him how he knew how to fix the computer. Todd told him he owned the same model and learned to repair it himself. The owner asked a few more questions and then, on the spur of the moment, offered thirteen-year-old Todd a job at his store. Todd was completely taken by surprise but accepted the offer. "I thought if nothing else, I could play computer games when business was slow," laughed Todd. This was the beginning of a mentor/apprentice partnership that benefitted both individuals.

The owner's snap decision paid off handsomely. Todd had an uncanny understanding of computers and computer games and could carry on intelligent conversations with anyone who entered the store. He was knowledgeable, confident, persuasive, and not intimidated by adults. Weekly sales increased and so did the owner's bank account. He had made a wise hire.

After two years of growth and profits, Todd approached the owner and requested a meeting. Todd shared his thoughts about the future of the gaming industry. "I told him the game business was changing," explained Todd. "The big stores were coming in and lowering prices. It was going to be difficult for a small store to compete with them." The owner admitted that, although the store was doing exceptionally well, he too was concerned about the future. Todd had a plan. "I suggested that we move into the website construction business," he said. The fifteen-year-old had the owner's attention. He asked Todd to continue with his thoughts.

Todd described how the World Wide Web was taking over the world of information, marketing and business. "Corporate America is going to need someone to build their websites," he told his boss. "Why not us?" The owner was interested initially, then even more so when Todd told him they would control pricing, something that could never happen in the game world. At the conclusion of Todd's presentation, the owner asked if there was a downside to the young man's business plan. Todd's reply caught the owner off guard: "It starts and ends with you and your lack of knowledge on how to build, sell, or service websites." Todd told his startled employer he could teach him everything he would need to know. Moving into website construction was not an easy decision for the store owner, but he trusted his teenage employee's ideas and took a chance.

Within a couple of years, the business expanded to five locations. Todd managed one of the stores. "I wore many hats," said Todd. "My responsibilities were managing employees, selling games and building websites." The game business remained profitable, but the store's primary source of income was website customers, including some Fortune 500 companies, hospitals, and privately-owned corporations. That business grew as Todd had predicted.

After six years of working and observing what it took to manage a successful business, Todd knew he wanted to someday start his own company and be his own boss. When it was time for college, he chose the University of Arizona and earned a Marketing and Business Management degree, a perfect complement to the entrepreneurial skills he developed working in the retail stores. After college, he returned to his hometown of Chicago to start a marketing company focused on website development and promotion. Todd named his company Envisionit Media Inc. and he drafted a business plan to present to potential lenders. He needed $50,000 to get started.

Todd started knocking on the doors of financial institutions to secure a loan. In spite of Todd's confidence and experience, he encountered a frustrating pattern of appointments and rejections. After more than twenty rejections, his quest for a loan became a test of will and endurance. His young age was working against him. Numerous bankers told him he was wasting his time and suggested he work for somebody until he had more experience.

I thought if nothing else I could play video games when business was slow.

"In spite of my frustrations," said Todd, "I had a goal and I wasn't giving up." Chicago is a big city with many banks so Todd kept knocking. His patience and persistence finally paid off when he met a loan officer who was impressed by Todd's enthusiasm as well as his business plan. He approved Todd's loan.

Todd opened Envisionit Media in February of 2003. He was the sole employee. Envisionit focused on brand development, graphic design, web design, and production. Todd was excellent at marketing and conveying to potential clients how Envisionit Media could deliver their corporate message to the world via the Internet. He closed sale after sale and soon created more work than he could process. With promises made and deadlines to be honored, Todd worked eighteen-hour days. He was mentally and physically exhausted, but there was a positive side to his relentless efforts. "I repaid my bank loan in eighteen months, which was years ahead of schedule," said Todd.

It was time to hire Envisionit's first employees. Todd was looking for someone smart with a strong work ethic and who would fit into the teamwork culture that Todd wanted to create at his company. He decided to tap into his circle of friends. "It was a risk," admitted Todd, "because I had been told never to mix business and friends." But Todd ignored the advice. He hired his friends and they brought along talents and skills that exceeded his own. Todd returned his focus to sales and marketing and Envisionit Media began to grow.

In an attempt to grow his company more quickly, Todd made a mistake that almost destroyed it. "I tried to speed up Envisionit's growth and bought a small advertising agency with expertise in radio, television, and print media," explained Todd. On paper it looked like a great acquisition but in reality it turned out quite differently. "I realized some of the ad agency employees lacked passion and were only working for a paycheck," recognized Todd. "I had worked hard to create a teamwork culture but now interoffice politics and self-promotion undermined the core values of my company." The depth of the problem became critical. Todd no longer enjoyed working in his own company. Something had to give.

Todd held a mandatory staff meeting on a Friday afternoon to discuss the problem. He posed a simple, thought-provoking question to his employees: "Why do you work at Envisionit Media?" The following week they would meet with Todd to discuss their answers.

After a week of meetings, most employees became refocused on the company's mission of providing great products and great service. Although Todd was tempted to fire employees who were not on the same page, he decided to "let nature takes its course." A number of employees that Todd had identified as "toxic" left on their own. The employees who stayed have become excellent assets to the company. "The acquisition experience was both stressful and valuable," reported Todd. "I learned the hard way that I did not want to be an advertising agency and sold off that piece of the company." Todd refocused his attention on building Envisionit Media into a first-class business.

Envisionit Media has now grown to over fifty employees and is a powerhouse in the world of internet marketing. They recently moved to a prime location in downtown Chicago. With an excellent reputation and core clientele including Toyota, Fairmont Hotel Chicago, Allstate, PayPal, Hyatt Hotels, and Jack Daniels, Envisionit is well positioned for continued robust growth.

I asked Todd what it felt like to achieve his American Dream at such a young age. "I have the good fortune to live in a country that encourages achievement," answered Todd. "I have always felt in control of my own destiny."

Are entrepreneurs born with the desire and drive to become successful, or are they created and molded into shape? Perhaps the answer is both. Maybe the drive is found in the gene pool and then it just needs the nurturing of others to bring it to life.

12
AN IMMIGRANT'S
PERSPECTIVE

Some kids have to grow up very fast. Durgesh "Doogs" Parbhoo was one of those kids. Doogs, of Indian decent, was born and raised in Johannesburg, South Africa, during the 1970s. He experienced prejudice in every aspect of his life. Blacks, Indians, and whites were separated by where they lived, where they went to school, and where they were allowed to shop, eat, and play.

By age nine, while kids in America were playing baseball, soccer, and basketball, Doogs was already working in the family business. His job was to sell women's stockings from a busy street corner in Johannesburg. The money he earned during the day helped to put food on the table that night. Doogs and his family lived in a 200-square-foot house with a piece of sheet metal for a roof. He and the other six family members slept on the floor.

Doogs encountered violence on the streets of Johannesburg on a daily basis. It was real, close to home, and a constant threat. By the age of fifteen, he had survived two knife attacks and multiple fights. Doogs told me he had witnessed over 100 people being assaulted—and some even murdered.

At nineteen, Doogs made a difficult decision. He left his family and friends and immigrated to the United States. He arrived in New York City in 1984 with $1,000 in his pocket. On his very first day in America, Doogs entered a restaurant to grab a bite to eat. "I will never forget that moment when the hostess seated me next to a table occupied by two white people," said Doogs, "That could never happen in South Africa." It became even more surreal when a white waiter took his order. Doogs finished his meal, paid his bill, and left a generous tip. "I was so excited and stunned about what had just happened," exclaimed Doogs. "I found a pay phone and called my family in Johannesburg to share my first experience in the United States."

Doogs left New York City for Canton, Ohio, where he had relatives who owned a motel and promised him employment. He cleaned rooms until he could find a better job.

Doogs eventually found a much better opportunity at a popular restaurant and bar named Bogarts. He was hired to wash dishes, bus tables, and tend bar. Bogarts was located next to my office and I was a lunchtime regular. That was where I first met Doogs and we became friends. I was impressed by his intelligence, work ethic, and positive attitude. I enjoyed learning about his life growing up in Johannesburg.

One day, Doogs and I got into a discussion about what motivated him to move to the United States. He replied that he based his decision to move to the States on three things: the freedom to vote, to have a voice in who and how the country was going to be run; an escape from the daily threat of violence; and the experience of the American Dream. "For me, the American Dream meant having the opportunity to become a business owner, raise a family, and own a home," explained Doogs.

Bogarts was a very popular place that could get crazy busy during peak hours, but Doogs always remained calm, in control, and enjoyed himself. I once asked Doogs how he maintained his cool in the midst of so much restaurant chaos. He replied, "Gary, my world has improved so much that it's hard for me to be anything but happy. I have a **He and the other six members of his family slept on the floor.** good job; I'm sleeping in a bed; I'm saving money; and I'm not under the threat of constant violence."

One of Doogs's goals was to own his own business. To prepare for that opportunity he started saving the money necessary to buy a business. Doogs received a significant boost in income when the owner of Bogart's promoted him to manager. He was now responsible for all aspects of running the restaurant. Doogs spent countless hours on the job, opening early for breakfast and closing late at night. It was not unusual for Doogs to spend the night sleeping in a booth so he would be there to open the doors in the morning. Any extra income Doogs earned went into his savings account.

Another key component of his American Dream involved marriage and raising a family. On a trip to visit family in Johannesburg, Doogs was introduced to Persina, a young woman who shared a similar drive and desire to live in the United States. After a two-week courtship they got married.

The immigration process was lengthy. It was a year before his new wife was able to join him in Canton. While Doogs continued to manage Bogarts, Persina worked two jobs. The couple worked long hours, saving their money to buy a business.

Doogs began exploring opportunities and eventually purchased a Mini-Mart convenience store in the nearby small town of Canal Fulton. The Parbhoos were the first Indian business owners in town and they were met with a prejudice they had not experienced since leaving South Africa. It was a side of America Doogs had not seen. A small minority of the regular clientele were very vocal about "foreigners" owning the store and stopped shopping there. The loss of sales caused some financial stress but it turned out to be a temporary setback. Fortunately the majority of the regulars welcomed the Parbhoos with open arms. Doogs made it a point to personally greet each customer and thank them for their support; it was impossible to ignore how happy and proud he was to be a business owner in America. His reputation spread quickly through the small town and an influx of new customers began shopping at the Mini-Mart.

Owning a home was still on Doog's goal list. The Parbhoos had started a family and were raising two daughters. Where to live and what type of home to buy was a big decision and the couple visited many homes and neighborhoods before making a selection. "We were so excited to purchase our first home," remembered Doogs. "It was truly a dream come true; it wasn't that long ago that I was sleeping on the floor in Johannesburg."

Even though Doogs never finished high school, education was always a top priority in the Parbhoo home. Both of his daughters are hardworking, excellent students who are pursuing careers in medicine. "It is absolutely incredible that my girls are going to be physicians," said Doogs. "The education opportunities are another reason America is a great country."

In a recent conversation, I pointed out to Doogs that based on his original goals, he had achieved his American Dream. He agreed, but said he is now focused on a new goal. "I have had so many good things happen to me and my family that I want to share my success." Doogs started by creating a new Christmas tradition at the Mini-Mart. "On Christmas—the busiest day of the year—I give the employees the day off. I open the store myself and work until midnight. At the close of business I add up the profits and split them among my employees. That bonus check has become a really big deal!"

In addition to his financial generosity, Doogs has started volunteering his time to help others less fortunate in his community. "I am a strong supporter of feeding the less fortunate. I have not forgotten what it was like selling stockings to help feed my own family," said Doogs. He also has not forgotten his relatives still living in South Africa. The cost of advanced education in Johannesburg is very high. Doogs started an education fund to help family members who wanted to continue with their schooling. "I just want to see how many people I can help achieve their dream like I achieved mine," he said.

[
Many people focus on the money side of the American Dream, but for Doogs it was all about freedom and quality of life.
]

13
AN ARTISTIC
PERSPECTIVE

What if your American Dream was to utilize the arts to rebuild a city? What would you do—and where would you start? Well, one thing you might consider doing is asking Robb Hankins what he would do.

Downtown Canton, Ohio, was a hub of activity during the 1950s and '60s. Restaurants, movie theaters, and major department stores were located in the heart of the city. As a kid, it was exciting to go downtown and be a part of the hustle and bustle. Canton had energy, the streets were full of people, and the city flourished. That all changed when Canton experienced the same phenomena that swept the nation: shopping malls in the suburbs. After the dust cleared, the city resembled a ghost town; the soul of Canton disappeared and with it went the lights and excitement I experienced in my youth. Empty storefronts became the norm. The only businesses that survived were government, banking, the judicial system, and a handful of bars and restaurants to serve the employees who still worked downtown.

There were attempts through the years to rebuild and refurbish Canton. Low rents attracted new restaurants and businesses. They would open with much fanfare and then close soon after due to a lack of patrons. On the positive side of the ledger, the Stark County Preservation Society became very proactive and fought to save some of the old office buildings scheduled to be demolished by the wrecking ball. The results of their efforts were beautifully refurbished landmarks that helped Canton maintain some of its past glory and identity.

One solution to revitalizing downtowns throughout the country was spurred by young professionals who wanted to live in an urban environment. Employment was a key piece to the puzzle. Unfortunately, the jobs necessary to support that type of revitalization were not plentiful in Canton. To reverse the future of the city something dramatic would have to happen, and it did.

A new sheriff came to town, metaphorically speaking. He did not come armed with a badge and a gun, but he came with a vision of what the arts could do to help reinvigorate downtown Canton. Robb Hankins was the "new sheriff" and he arrived following a national search to replace the president and CEO of the local arts association, ArtsinStark. The forty-five-year-old nonprofit is responsible for an annual fund drive that raises money to support the city's arts organizations. The board of directors was looking for a leader who could grow the fund drive and lengthen the reach of the arts community to include all of Stark County. The selection process was lengthy. Numerous qualified candidates had applied for the position. Fortunately, the selection committee chose wisely and Robb Hankins was hired. His energy, fresh perspective and enthusiasm brought a can-do attitude to the arts community.

The first time I met Robb was at a "Welcome to Canton" cocktail party. On my way to the event, I remember thinking what a challenging job this individual had accepted. Upon being introduced to Robb, I wished him a sincere "Good luck." To which he replied: "My job has nothing to do with luck. It is all about hard work, preparation and passion and I have brought that with me to Canton. I have a plan and I am well prepared for the challenges of my new position." I have to admit I was a bit taken aback, but I admired his confidence. At the time, I thought he might not be fully aware of the obstacles he faced going forward. It did not take me long to realize I had underestimated Robb.

Robb came to Canton with an impressive resume in the non-profit arts management world. He had been involved with arts organizations in Long Beach, California; Eugene, Oregon; and Hartford, Connecticut. His experience gave him an understanding of the issues facing both the local arts and business community and gave his vision for Canton credibility. His master plan was a compelling blend of passion and common sense that painted a very encouraging picture of what could happen in Canton if the community embraced the arts.

Robb's arrival coincided with one of the most successful art exhibits to ever find its way to Canton. Prior to Robb's hire, the local art museum had booked *Kimono as Art: The Landscapes of Itchiku Kabota*. The exhibit was a coup for Canton. The only other stop for the collection of hand-sewn silk kimonos was San Diego. The exhibit exceeded expectations. The kimonos were spectacular! Rave reviews brought 100,000 people to the museum. The local economic impact was measured in millions of dollars. Kimono set the stage for Robb to further engage the community in support of the arts.

Since Robb's arrival, the annual arts drive has experienced steady growth. The campaign prior to Robb taking the helm had topped out at $970,000. In 2015, the campaign set and met a goal of $1,775,000. The unprecedented growth and additional dollars provided by the fund drive gives ArtsinStark the ability to award grants for arts projects in all parts of the county. When I questioned

It did not take me long to realize that I had underestimated Robb.

him about the success of the drive, he replied, "I love the idea of small places that do really big things."

One of the first items on Robb's revitalization agenda was the establishment of an arts district in downtown Canton. The Canton Chamber of Commerce and ArtsinStark joined forces to turn an eight-block section of the city into a dedicated art area. The goal was to provide low-rent spaces for artists to open studios and galleries, creating destinations for people to visit. Robb's vision was exciting but, with only one established gallery in the eight blocks, he was greeted with skepticism. On a mission, Robb met with landlords and artists and explained how an arts district had worked in other cities. After countless meetings, Robb persuaded the landlords to establish reasonable rents and convinced local artists to rent the spaces. Today, twenty-six art galleries and studios operate in the district.

To further establish an identity for the new arts area, Robb, with the support of the Chamber of Commerce, began commissioning and placing public art by local artists throughout the district. "We used public art as a billboard to show that something was happening in the new arts district," said Robb. "When you see art," he explained, "you know you are in the right place." Three-dimensional wall art, murals, and sculptures began to appear throughout the eight designated blocks. More than fifty pieces of art now grace the city streets—with many more to come.

A significant challenge was how to encourage people to visit the arts district and support the artists? The answer was to throw a monthly party, an idea that Robb borrowed from other cities. ArtsinStark launched First Friday, a street party based on arts, music, and food held the first Friday of every month, regardless of the weather. Like anything new, it took time to catch on, but with strong press and clever programming, including ice sculpture contests, chalk art, and street concerts, First Friday attendance has steadily increased. Travel downtown on any first Friday and you will find the streets buzzing with people, live music on every corner, and restaurants and art galleries packed with patrons. To date, over 100 First Fridays have brought thousands of visitors to downtown Canton.

Following the establishment of the Canton Arts District, Robb was asked what needed to happen next for Canton to become a viable city. "Downtown Canton is ready for downtown living. Creative people live in creative places. If we had fifty new units suitable for young professionals, empty nesters, and just regular folks, we could rent them out tomorrow. We are going to start creating these properties. After we fill the first fifty, we are going to keep right on going. When we are done, every weekend in downtown Canton will start feeling like a First Friday."

Robb's predictions have been accurate. As soon as landlords finished renovating apartments, they were rented. Last year, the Onesto, a once grand hotel built in 1930, was reopened as luxurious apartments. Renamed The Onesto Lofts, all forty-two units are now occupied. Today, over 100 apartments have been refurbished and leased in downtown Canton. Many more are under construction and on the drawing board.

Robb's original action plan was to bring the arts into every county school system. National studies have shown that including arts as part of school curriculum improves student performance in all subjects. That being said, Robb wanted local proof. ArtsinStark funded pilot programs in three different grade schools and named the initiative the SmArts Program. One of the original test programs was introduced at the Gorrel Elementary school. Both a dancer and a visual artist became resident artists for a fourth grade class. The idea was to translate reading and math assignments into art experiences. At the conclusion of the first year, average reading scores had improved by two percent in fourth grade classes that did not have an arts-based program. On the contrary, classrooms participating in the SmArts class found scores improved by an amazing twenty-three percent. Similar results occurred at the other two pilot schools and SmArts was off and running. After three years of trials, students participating in SmArts programs scored substantially higher than non-participants. These results were reported to the community and provided a boost in fundraising. Parents, whose children had not been part of the test programs, demanded their children become involved in SmArts. Today, all seventeen school districts in Stark County have incorporated the SmArts Program into their classrooms.

Arts and the National Football League? What might seem like an odd pairing to some was a natural fit to Robb. Canton is the proud home of the Professional Football Hall of Fame. The Hall is the crown jewel of the county (and state) tourism industry, drawing fans from all over the world. The Pro Football Hall of Fame annual induction ceremonies have turned into a multi-week event, highlighted by the Concert for Legends, the induction of the newest class of players, and the first pre-season NFL football game of the year. If you are a football fan you'll find it is quite an exciting few weeks. Robb and a small group of

ArtsinStark board members were discussing the Hall of Fame's importance to Canton and possible ways to incorporate football into the arts district.

In 2014 Robb approached the Hall of Fame with his idea of artfully depicting the eleven most significant moments in football history and displaying the artwork throughout downtown Canton. The Hall of Fame was receptive to the idea and asked the NFL to identify the eleven most important events in the history of the game. Robb and his committee sent out a national request for artist proposals. "The Eleven" is the most ambitious undertaking ever attempted by ArtsinStark and required funding in the neighborhood of $2.2 million. Over $1 million has already been raised. The first two pieces are sculptures. *Birth of the NFL 1920* by Michael Clapper was unveiled in 2014 during the Hall of Fame. The second piece, *The NFL Draft*, 1936, was created by Gail Folwell and was unveiled the following year. As Robb says, "When finished, there will be eleven more reasons for football fans to visit downtown Canton."

In 2015, ArtsinStark received the prestigious Governor's Award and Robb Hankins signed a new three-year contract to remain as President and CEO of ArtsinStark. I asked Robb how he felt about his many accomplishments. He looked me square in the eye and answered, "Gary, I am happy with the progress but there is still a ton of work to be done. I have big-time goals and I have not met them. My dream is to utilize arts as the cornerstone of the rebirth of Canton. I have a great start but so much more to accomplish."

With his impressive track record, I am excited to find out what Robb has been dreaming about for the future.

For Canton to move forward it took someone from the outside, someone with a vision, a relentless work ethic and an incredible passion to succeed.

14
A GENERAL'S PERSPECTIVE

U nited States Army Brigadier General Kaffia "Belle" Jones is a woman who has lived and breathed the American Dream. Belle says her achievements in life—she also holds a doctorate in psychology and is a licensed Clinical Psychologist—can be traced directly back to her humble roots in the small community of Beaufort County, South Carolina, and her upbringing by her grandmother, Mrs. Carrie Jefferson.

In 1926, Mrs. Jefferson paid $25 for five acres of land in Dale, South Carolina—pretty impressive considering what $25 buys today. Her young husband had died and she used the death benefit proceeds from his life insurance policy to buy the property. The acreage became the Jefferson's home, family compound, and a refuge for Belle.

Mrs. Jefferson's daughter, Mary L. Melvin, was the divorced mother of Belle and her five siblings. Dale was a good place to raise a family but not so good when it came to finding suitable employment. The jobs there did not pay enough to support six children, so, reluctantly, Mary left her family with their grandmother and relocated to Teaneck, New Jersey, where she cleaned homes during the day and worked the night shift at a factory. She sent money to her mother for the care of her children and began saving so she could move her family to New Jersey.

Belle was raised by her grandmother for the first sixteen years of her life. Mrs. Jefferson was strict, tough, and believed in discipline. She taught her granddaughter to be fair, firm, consistent, and to always hold her space. Mrs. Jefferson also had a kind and generous heart. "My grandmother had a soft spot for abandoned children," said Belle. "Our home was often full to overflowing with kids who had nowhere else to go. In many ways my grandmother ran an orphanage and she did it with virtually no money. Somehow she made it work. To this day, I have no idea how she did it."

Eventually, Belle was able to join her mother in Teaneck. She finished high school there, enrolled at a local business school, and earned a certificate in basic secretarial skills. She also met and married a young Army man. "I wasn't really sure what I wanted to do in life but that changed one day when I stopped at the local post office to mail a package," said Belle. "The line was long and moving very slowly. I was bored to death. So I started reading the advertising posters on the walls and one grabbed my attention."

The poster that caught her attention belonged to the New Jersey National Guard. It read: *If you want to be somebody, become a part of something, make a difference in your life and give back to your country, Join the New Jersey National Guard.* Something clicked for Belle and she enrolled the next day.

Although Belle enlisted in the New Jersey National Guard, she transferred to the South Carolina Guard and attended Basic Training at Fort Jackson. At the same time, her husband was relocated to Fort Ord, California. She joined him after completing her basic training and enlisted in the California National Guard. Belle knew she wanted to become an officer. In order to do that, she needed to enroll in the California Military Academy. Before she could do that, she needed a college associate degree, so she began taking classes at Monterey Peninsula College, a two-year university.

With total confidence and professional poise the inmates understood that I had zero tolerance for their infringing on my space.

Unfortunately Belle's marriage ended in divorce and she was left with the responsibility of raising two sons. She completed her associate's degree, entered the Military Academy, and took a secretarial job at a Culligan Water franchise. Even though she was promoted to office manager, the job did not pay her enough to support her family.

One of Belle's sisters lived in nearby Seaside, California, and worked as a Correctional Officer at the Correctional Training Facility, Soledad. She told Belle the prison had job openings and paid a very good salary. To work there, Belle needed to be certified by the California Peace Officer Academy. After completing that program, Belle was hired at Soledad. Her new job solved her financial problems but with it came a brand new learning curve. She now needed to figure out out how to manage life as a correctional officer.

She was tested on the job. "I walked across the prison yard and was immediately surrounded by inmates," explained Belle. "They were blocking my path, which, according to my Peace Officer training, should not be tolerated. I held my space, kept walking and talking to them. With total confidence and professional poise, the inmates understood that I had zero tolerance for them infringing on my space. They backed off and I kept moving." To prevent future problems and counteract any misunderstandings, Belle adopted a personal zero-tolerance policy. It did not take long for it to get tested.

Interestingly, it was not the inmates who tested Belle's policy or posed her biggest threat; it was the male correctional officers. "They were disrespectful, always whistling at me and making in-appropriate comments," Belle said. "They stopped bothering me when they found out that I could, and would, stand up to them."

Because communication between correctional officers and inmates was critical for stability in the prison, Belle created her own protocol based on her secretarial experience. "I informed the prisoners that if they wanted to have a discussion or had a request, they had to make an appointment," she said. She posted a schedule and inmates could sign up for time slots whenever they wanted them. Belle's fellow guards thought it would never work. They were wrong. "The idea came from my secretarial experiences," said Belle. "If someone wanted to see my boss they couldn't just drop in. They made an appointment." Belle's new system also came with rules. The inmates had to line up in single file and remain quiet. If an inmate ignored the rules, Belle removed him from the schedule. Her fellow correctional officers soon followed suit and adopted Belle's system.

Life as a correctional officer provided a nice income but working with inmates did little for Belle's social life. She found a solution to her problem in the military. "It was a godsend," she said. "I found common ground with fellow members of the military. I liked what they believed in: hard work, discipline, a strong sense of camaraderie, and country. It just felt right."

In 1980, Belle was commissioned as a Second Lieutenant from the Military Academy. "That rank provided a huge upgrade in my social life," said Belle. "I was entitled to membership in The Officer's Club. It was a dream come true for me. I attended formal dinners and developed life-long friendships with like-minded soldiers. I even learned how to ballroom dance!" After three more years with the National Guard of California, Belle transferred to the Army Reserve for her first Commander assignment.

Meanwhile, Belle continued her civilian education at Saybrook University, earning a Bachelor of Arts degree and Master's and Doctorate degrees in Psychology. She wrote her dissertation on the treatment of black veterans following World War II, a topic relatively unknown to many Americans. Many black servicemen chose to return to Europe after processing out of the military. Belle wanted to know why. She traveled to Europe and interviewed the expatriates. The reasons she was given were both disturbing and enlightening. One veteran told Belle, "I wanted to be treated like a human being." Even though these soldiers had risked their lives for their country, they still faced racial prejudice in America. In Western Europe, they were treated with dignity, appreciation, and respect, making the decision to live there much easier. Belle's dissertation told the black veterans' stories and earned her a Doctorate in Psychology.

In 2004, after twenty-five years of service, Belle retired from the California Department of Corrections. She had no intention of kicking back in retirement and taking it easy. Belle shifted her focus to the Army Reserves and took a much more active role. She began accepting assignments in numerous locations around the world. One of her tours of duty was a one-year stint in Afghanistan, which Belle extended into a two-year stay. Belle explained, "I requested a one-year extension because I am a US soldier first and foremost and my mission was not finished. Leaving something unfinished was absolutely unacceptable."

Belle's promotions through the US Army ranks culminated on September 18, 2012, when she was promoted to the impressive

THE AMERICAN DREAM REVISITED

rank of Brigadier General in honor of her exemplary leadership, dedication, and distinguished service to the United States Army. Belle was the fifth black female to achieve that honor. As a Brigadier General, she was responsible for thousands of troops stationed all over the world. Belle also quickly realized a pressure she had not anticipated; she had become a role model in the eyes of black soldiers. "I was humbled and honored to be in such a position," said Belle.

Belle retired from the Army in 2015 which gave her time to pursue her other passions. She opened a private clinical psychology practice in Monterey and she began spending more time on developing the family property in South Carolina. "My family inherited the Jefferson Family Compound from my grandmother in 1995," said Belle. "It is the place I return to when I need a break from the stresses of my chosen careers."

Belle began purchasing land that was adjacent to her grand-mother's original five acres. The process was painstakingly slow. In many ways it turned into a title and land research project. Belle's diligence uncovered the names of the various owners of the surrounding rural acreage. She tracked them down across the country, informed them of their ownership interests and pur-chased as much property as she could afford.

In 2001, Belle formed The Indian Hill Land Development Company, named after the slave plantation that once occupied the land. The original purpose of the company was to protect the family compound from being surrounded by other land develop-ments. It has since developed into something much more.

The Indian Hill Land Development Company has since purchased over sixty acres surrounding the Jefferson family compound. Belle has divided the land into lots, dug wells, built roads, and marketed the property to a unique group of potential buyers. "I have directed my marketing and sales efforts toward the descendants of the slaves who worked the fields," explained Belle. She reports that many families have returned to the area. Belle offers them the opportunity to do so by providing affordable housing. In many ways, Belle, via Indian Hill, is helping people achieve their American Dream by providing home ownership opportunities. As an avid supporter of the local community, she is continuing her grandmother's legacy.

I am quite sure Belle's grandmother, Mrs. Carrie Jefferson, would be extremely proud of her granddaughter's military and civilian achievements. And, no doubt, she would be amazed by the number of families who are benefitting from her $25 real estate investment.

[
It really is quite incredible how a simple poster hanging in a post office could have been the starting point for Belle's remarkable journey.
]

15
MY PERSPECTIVE

S o, there you have it. Thirteen different perspectives. Thirteen stories of ordinary people achieving extraordinary results. It doesn't matter where you come from. It doesn't matter what color skin you have. It doesn't matter when you were born. All that matters is what you do with the possibilities that surround you.

Thomas Edison said, "Opportunity is missed by most people because it is dressed in overalls and looks like work." There are no shortcuts but there are a handful of strategies, lessons, attitudes, and roadmaps that can help guide you to your American Dream. Here are seven strategies I have discovered in this pursuit:

1. **First and foremost is to determine what your personal dream is.** It may be similar to one I've includ-

ed in this book or it could be radically different. Whatever it happens to be, the important thing is you have to figure it out. Because then and only then will you be able to apply the lessons in this book to help you achieve your dream.

I wish there were more I could do to help you discover what your own American Dream is—but I can't. It's one of those important questions that only you can answer. There is no book or magic formula to follow. The best suggestion I can give you is to ask yourself some serious questions: What excites you?

Is it art? Music? Politics? Business? Sports? Military? Honestly, whatever your personal answer is doesn't matter as long as it lights your fire. Because, in case you missed it, American Dreams are not given and they aren't based on entitlement. They are earned. After you determine your dream, write it down and keep it where you can see it on a daily basis.

2. **There is going to be frustration.** There is going to be disappointment. At times you will want to give up, but don't. Nothing happens overnight. Failure is just the word we use to describe the process of learning to be successful. This is the second lesson of the book. Call it grit, determination, or perseverance. Whatever you choose to name it, this might be the single most important lesson. The people I wrote about pursued their passions. They refused to quit. For you to accomplish your dream you will need to adopt the same relentless attitude.

Remember, whether it's gang life on the streets of the Bronx, a learning disability in the suburbs, or the atrocities of war—there will be difficulties. And sometimes, in those darkest moments, the only fuel you'll have is the passion of your Dream and your "I will not quit" attitude.

3. **Successful entrepreneurs have an ability to remember where they came from, both literally and figuratively.** For those dark days when you feel frustrated by a lack of progress, take a moment and reflect. Instead of looking forward to see how far you have to go, change directions and look backward to measure where you started from and see how far you have come. This exercise can provide a much needed boost to your self-esteem and keep you moving in the proper direction.

4. **Remember—you do not have to do this alone.** Every person in this book had a mentor or two who helped and guided them toward their dreams.

Sometimes they are teachers or community leaders. Sometimes they are parents or neighbors, and sometimes they are fictional characters. Again, it doesn't matter where you find your mentor, just make sure you do.

It's a big, connected world out there and chances are someone has done what you are trying to do. Reach out to them. Send them an email. Call their office. Write a letter. Most people love to help others, especially if they see traces of themselves in the people asking for assistance.

5. **Lighten up and have a sense of humor—especially about yourself and your circumstances.** Take a page from Dr. Stabholz's book. If people starving to death in the concentration camps of World War II were able to make light of their situation by playing "Find the Potato" in the soup, then surely you can find humor in your situation too. The ability to laugh at your mistakes and learn from them is a game changer. Sometimes you just have to smile, shake your head and move on.

6. **Don't be afraid to follow your intuition.** You don't have to say prayers to King Solomon or go for wintery walks. But do listen to your inner voice. Not the one that's full of negativity and doubt, but the one that's a confident and powerful source of inspiration.

7. **Give back.** It's no coincidence this book started in a coffee shop called Karma. Helping others along the way is important. Generosity is a cornerstone of every individual in this book. Once you achieve your American Dream it will be up to you to carry the torch and help when asked. Whether it is money, services, or plain old advice, it is up to you to pay it forward. Remember to be thankful and grateful for the good you already have in your life and be sure to share it with those who could use a bit more in theirs.

Keep striving and never give up on the pursuit of your American Dream. I believe that you, too, can make your American Dream your American reality!

Epilogue
A KARMIC
PERSPECTIVE

I am often fascinated by how the world works, especially the part when life sometimes just comes together by chance, by divine intervention or by whatever you choose to believe. For example, I think back to my first day at Miami University and how I happened to become an English major. That seemingly random decision eventually led me to Professor Denham's class and served as my introduction to the American Dream.

Or perhaps the morning I was sipping my mocha at Karma Café and the table of college students sat behind me going off on the American Dream. If my timing or theirs were not perfect I would have never written *The American Dream Revisited*. But that is not what happened. Those students rekindled a fire in me that had turned to smoldering ashes.

I recently found myself back at Karma Cafe, sipping my mocha and thinking about how college had been a launching point for me. It was freedom, and my first opportunity to make decisions and begin to shape my own life. I found my first mentors and learned about goal setting and how to communicate with my fellow students and teachers. Most importantly it was also where I met my wife, Linda. Without question, college played a major role in achieving my American Dream.

Because college was life-changing for me, I decided to establish The American Dream Revisited Scholarship in partnership with Scholarship Management Resources. For every copy of *The American Dream Revisited* sold, I will donate twenty percent of the profits to fund The American Dream Revisited Scholarship. This scholarship will provide support to college students across the country who have financial need and are majoring in Entrepreneurial Studies and/or have displayed entrepreneurial tendencies. To apply for The American Dream Revisited Scholarship or to seek more information, please visit www.ofic.org/smr/americandreamrevisited.

Thank you for purchasing this book; together we can make a difference.

ACKNOWLEDGEMENTS

A number of people played a part in helping me reach the finish line for this book, but absolutely no one came close to the effort my wife Linda put into this project. She kept me going when I was frustrated, stuck by me, and provided great editing. Thank you Linda!

Thank you to my son Max, a gifted writer in his own right. He helped me keep everything in perspective in more ways than you can imagine.

My gratitude to my life-long friend Barry Adelman for pointing out the not-so-obvious to me, and my father Stan Sirak for being my American Dream role model. Thank you to Dan Sullivan of Strategic Coach for inspiring me to write books. I also very much appreciate the friendship of David Katz and Jim Jelinek and their countless conversations and encouragement. Thank you Denise Gotchall for my introduction to Belle Jones, Sarah Ructtecki for her support and assistance with Todd Brook's story, and Laura Tsangos for her insights into Amish culture. I also wish to thank W. Brian Furnish of Miami University for his research regarding Professor Denham.

I appreciate the employees at Sirak Financial Services for their constant encouragement: Carolyn Snyder, Lisa Fleming, Linda Smith, Jeff Sirak, Jennifer Cassidy, Farris Martin, Tara

Humston, and especially Raquel Thompson for being my go-to person on this project.

Thank you to Jeff Walker, author of *Launch*, for his introduction to David Hancock. Thank you David Hancock, President of Morgan James Publishing, for your strong support, Stephanie McLawhorn for your assistance in finishing this project, and Anna Floit at The Peacock Quill for your editing skills.

Thank you to Ryan Humbert for designing the cover, the written words by John Armato, and photographer Angie Skotnicky for my cover photo.

A very special thank you to Becky Duplain and Walt Stanislawski of the Paul and Carol David Foundation for their advice regarding scholarships and to Gordon Brollier, President of the Foundation of Independent Colleges, for his assistance in helping me design and establish the American Dream Revisited Scholarship.

My final thank you goes to Jim Blasingame, founder and President of the Small Business Advocate, for writing the forward to *The American Dream Revisited*.

Scholarship
Management Resources
www.ofic.org/smr/americandreamrevisited

ABOUT THE AUTHOR

Gary Sirak is an author, entrepreneur, public speaker, financial advisor and American Dream advocate. He is the President of Sirak Financial Services, Inc., a family-owned company. For the past 35 years, he has consulted with entrepreneurs to help build, grow and sustain their businesses.

To learn more about achieving your American Dream today, check out GarySirak.com for a Free bonus chapter. It can help you get started and provide a scorecard to measure your progress.

GarySirak.com

A free eBook edition is available with the purchase of this book.

To claim your free eBook edition:

1. Download the Shelfie app.
2. Write your name in upper case in the box.
3. Use the Shelfie app to submit a photo.
4. Download your eBook to any device.

Shelfie
A free eBook edition is available
with the purchase of this print book.

CLEARLY PRINT YOUR NAME ABOVE IN UPPER CASE

Instructions to claim your free eBook edition:
1. Download the Shelfie app for Android or iOS
2. Write your name in **UPPER CASE** above
3. Use the Shelfie app to submit a photo
4. Download your eBook to any device

Print & Digital Together Forever.

Snap a photo

Free eBook

Read anywhere

The Morgan James
Speakers Group

↗ www.TheMorganJamesSpeakersGroup.com

We connect Morgan James published
authors with live and online events
and audiences whom will benefit
from their expertise.

Morgan James makes all of our titles available
through the Library for All Charity Organization.

www.LibraryForAll.org